Dedication

To Keri Jones, Noralv Askeland, and Chandrakant Chavada, "…outstanding among the apostles."

In loving memory of Hazel, 1943–2002, "prepared as a bride…for her husband."

Endorsements

The *Lion and the Lamb* is not an easy book to put down! Prepare for late nights if you open this Holy Spirit–inspired read.

Simon Rowland
Chief executive

Tony Ling's passion and profound insight into the whole counsel of God's Word enables him to paint the big picture of God's eternal plan, and our place in it, with great richness and clarity. He makes connections and draws parallels that make your jaw drop—not just because you have never seen them before, but because once he has painted the picture for you, it seems so obvious!

Chris Hamer-Hodges
Software engineer

So often the Book of Revelation is either forgotten, distorted, or simply just ignored because it is too difficult to understand—yet Christians in every generation must grasp its powerful message. To help today's church, Tony Ling provides an insightful guide to John's letter of faith and hope with a prophetic understanding deeply rooted in the rest of Scripture.

Hugh Griffiths
Church leader, Wales, UK

This is an encouraging read from beginning to end! It's full of practical teaching of who we are in Christ Jesus—and inspiring us to live as overcomers and conquerors, demonstrating the power of God in our lives.

Sharon Key
Secretary

Tony's first volume is so easy to read and suggests practical responses to the Word of God: it emphasizes the centrality of the risen Jesus on the throne and reminds me of the Church's purpose in our world.

John Rigby
Church deacon

Having read *The Lion and the Lamb* four times, one finds oneself fascinated and thrilled with the new revelation that it is all about Jesus. His centrality removes any unnecessary attention on the antichrist or the beast, and it brings a fresh understanding of God's plan for our daily life now and in the future.

Ted Kent
Veteran missionary to Africa

In *The Lion and the Lamb* Tony Ling opens the Book of Revelation in a way that is both encouraging and deeply inspiring. He helps us to appreciate how Revelation, which is as relevant today as it was then, continues to change lives through its wonderful message of overcoming faith and unwavering hope. I highly recommend this insightful and compelling book.

Bill Clark
Church leader, Canada

The Lion and the Lamb is one of those rare books that I could not put down but had to finish. I believe this book will have a profound impact as it gets itself into the hands of people all over the world. Thank you for obeying the Holy Spirit and writing an outstanding book that helps us better understand the Book of Revelation while making it so applicable for everyday living!

Jim Harkins
Church leader, USA

Tony Ling removes all the confusion and fear from the Book of Revelation and keeps the focus where it belongs—on Jesus!

Allan Hinchliffe
Manager

Tony Ling's clear insight into the Book of Revelation has simply deepened my appreciation of Jesus.

Veronica Elliot
Grandmother

I love the way Tony Ling takes our eyes off trivial earthly things and fixes them on heavenly realities. The book brings a life-changing blast of fresh spiritual vision.

Alison Lloyd
Youth and community worker

This book spoke volumes to me, helping me see the Book of Revelation in a different light. It filled me with joy, as I have never read a book full of so much passion before.

Joyce McNamara
Mother and grandmother

This book is a deep well of wisdom and inspiration. It is a superb reference for those who want more from God.

Chris Lake
Community worker

Contents

Introduction 11

Chapter 1
Incense—Prayers 13

Chapter 2
A Prophetic People 31

Chapter 3
The Flood from the Abyss 51

Chapter 4
The Unholy Trinity 69

Chapter 5
The Heavenly Woman 81

Chapter 6
The Exodus Paradigm 101

Chapter 7
In the Winepress 117

Chapter 8
Babylon Fallen, Part 1 131

Chapter 9
Babylon Fallen, Part 2 145

Chapter 10
Enter the Bride 161

Chapter 11
The Return of the Rider 173

Chapter 12
The Millennium 187

Chapter 13
The Holy City 201

Introduction

In this volume of *The Lion and the Lamb,* we conclude our current reflections on the book of Revelation. As stated in the introduction to Volume 1, this is not a commentary, nor is it an exhaustive treatment of the biblical text. Not every passage, image, or concept within John's prophecy has been examined or explained. What some may think of as less significant verses have been given more space than others that might be considered to be of greater importance. However, in this work I have honestly and humbly sought to address some of the major issues relevant to the Church of Jesus Christ in the twenty-first century and to individual saints of God—those redeemed by His blood and sealed by His Spirit—who are its members. For it is here, among the people to whom the Book of Revelation is addressed—people like you and me—that the work of God's cosmic redemption begins and reaches its glorious climax.

> *"If anyone is in Christ he is a new creation; the old has gone, the new has come!"* (2 Corinthians 5:17)
>
> *"The old order of things has passed away. . . I am making everything new!"* (Revelation 21:4-5)

CHAPTER 1

Incense—Prayers

In this chapter, we are going to look at the incense altar and first place it in its prophetic context. Chapters 10 and 11 of the Book of Revelation are like a prophetic interlude. They reveal how John gets recommissioned into his prophetic ministry.

When Jesus called his disciples together and made them apostles, they ministered through different giftings and different anointings. You cannot describe an apostle outside of gifting, anointing, and ministry. The three disciples who were in the most intimate relationship with Jesus in his earthly ministry, the three that had access to secrets that others were excluded from, were Simon, James, and John. James and John were brothers, and, like Simon, they were fishermen. They had other things in common also: they were from the same town, they worked in the same industry, and they were business partners.

Sons of Thunder

The other thing that these three men had in common is that they had their names changed. We know that Jesus called Simon "Peter," and in saying "upon this rock I will build my church," he gives us a little insight into the nature of all apostolic ministries and foundational gifts to his church. James and John also had their names changed; he called them "Boanerges," which literally means "sons of thunder." Some people say that they were called "sons of thunder" because they went around making a lot of noise, shouting and hollering, and that they were a bit wayward. Actually, it has nothing to do with how loud they were. Throughout Scripture, one of the images for the voice of God, and for prophetic declaration, is thunder. These two men were probably called "sons of thunder" because they were anointed with a prophetic gift.

We see the prophetic gift in both James and John. James was the first of the disciples to die for his faith, and he was killed, it tells us, by the sword, which is the classic way of prophets dying. Elijah, when he is complaining to God about the state of the nation, says, "*The Israelites have rejected Your covenant, broken down Your altars, and put Your prophets to death with the sword*" (1 Kings 19:10). To be put to death with the sword is a prophet's death. James was put to death by the sword and was therefore numbered among those whose voices were crying from under the altar. I wonder sometimes if John, as he heard those cries, recognized his brother's voice! He is still speaking, though he is dead. John, of course, goes on to be the author of the only prophetic book that we have in the New Testament; he is clearly a prophet.

He is recommissioned here in this chapter to prophesy again: "*You must prophesy again*" (Rev. 10:11). Remember, we have considered that he is quite aged by now. He is probably quite elderly, but God recommissions him into a new task of prophetic ministry that is going to touch the ends of the earth and all the kingdoms of the world. As part of that ministry, John records,

> *I was given a reed like a measuring rod* (Revelation 11:1a).

Now one of the tasks for prophets in the Old Testament was to measure or to align. They are often seen with either a measuring line or a plumb line because they determine whether something is straight and conformed to the will and purpose of God. That is one of the ministries of prophets. They see if things are lined up with God's purpose. They see if things are righteous and straight. They measure and make sure that what we are building conforms to the pattern that has been shown to them on the mountain. That is part of their job, part of the prophetic ministry. And so John, in the recommissioning of his prophetic gift, is given a measuring rod and is told, "*Go and measure the temple of God and the altar* [of incense], *and count the worshipers there*" (Rev. 11:1b). But he is also told, "*But exclude the outer court; do not measure it, because it has been given to the Gentiles. They will trample on the holy city for 42 months*" (Rev. 11:2). John's prophetic word is going to bring a separation between the Holy Place (which is where the altar of incense is and the true worshipers of God are) and the Outer Court, which is being given to the Gentiles.

The Outer Court

The interesting thing about this, of course, is that the Outer Court of the temple was known as the "Court of the Gentiles." That was the only place that Gentiles were allowed to come. Paul got into trouble because people said that he was taking Gentiles right into the temple. They were only allowed into the Outer Court, and, in fact, in every passageway that took you further toward the heart of the temple there were signs forbidding Gentiles to enter, and if they disobeyed, they would be put to death. So this temple area, this outer court, which was open to everybody, was known as the Court of the Gentiles. This is where the God-fearers could come. This is where the people who wanted to know something about God, to have some teaching and revelation, to see something of the glory of the temple, could come.

Of course, the tragedy of this Court of the Gentiles was that this was the very place that the Jews had turned into a market. This was the very place where the moneychangers sat. So the Gentiles coming to seek God would come into this Outer Court and find it not only like a marketplace but, as Jesus called it, like a den of robbers. This was not a good testimony, but this is what Israel had become. Rather than a provocation and an inspiration to the nations, they had become an offense to the nations. Paul actually writes in one of his letters that the name of God was blasphemed among the nations because of the behavior of those who should have been God's covenant people (see Rom. 2:24). It is Jesus who comes into this Court of the Gentiles and is provoked to anger by all that is going on. He makes a whip, kicks over the tables, drives out the animals, makes a huge commotion, and insists, "*My house will be called a house of prayer for all nations*" (Mark 11:17). That is what it is supposed to be. But the place where all nations can come is no longer a house of prayer; it is house of merchandise. It is no longer a house where you receive from God; it is a house where you are fleeced by God's people.

God tells John that the Outer Court is going to be handed over to the Gentiles—there is some justice there—to be trampled underfoot. What he is saying is that the time has arrived in the unfolding of God's purpose where Israel, ethnic Israel, is going to meet its ultimate rejection by the trampling down of the physical temple. And when Israel was overcome by the Roman invasion in A.D. 70, not one stone of the temple was left standing. It was utterly destroyed. But God says to John that those who occupy the place of worship, those who are at the altar, are to be measured in an inclusive way. That is, they belong to God. They are not going to be harmed. It is only those who have not obeyed the Lord who will come to harm. Jesus went into the temple and said, "*My house will be a house of prayer*" (Luke 19:46), but when he finally rejects ethnic Israel he says, "*Your house is left to you desolate*" (Matt. 23:38). It is as if he is saying, "It was My house but now it is your house and, if you want it, you can have it; but I tell you, it is going to be desolate."

The Burning of Incense

All those who were reckoned to be true believers were preserved, kept for God, measured, and gathered for prayer around the altar. That altar is the altar of incense. It represents prayer. One of the things that we desperately need to rediscover in the churches in our day is how to pray. Some of us have elders who gather together or leaders who gather together or prayer meetings that everyone is invited to, but nobody turns up to. We all have those kinds of prayer meetings, but God is looking for a church that knows how to pray. I am convinced, I am unshakably convinced, that the main function of the temple in the Old Testament was prayer. I will tell you why I believe that. Nowhere in the Scriptures can I find the temple called a house of sacrifice. Nowhere in the Scriptures can I find the temple called a house of ceremony. Nowhere in the Scriptures can I find the temple called a house of priestly function. But I do find it called this: a house of prayer. "*My house will be called a house of prayer for all nations*" (Isa. 56:7). That is what God speaks through Isaiah the prophet. All the furniture of the temple, like everything else in creation and in God's revelation, everything was arranged to show us something of God.

Here is an illustration: picture yourself in the days of Eli the priest. There are no visions. There are no prophecies. The Word of God has been hushed. It is neglected. It is rare. There is one little boy asleep in the temple. And then God breaks through, just before the lamp goes out. Before utter and total darkness comes, God raises up a young man to be a prophet in the nation. That lamp in the temple is a picture of God's prophetic word. We will pick that up later on. The bread that was laid out speaks to us of a God who meets all our needs. The Ark of the Covenant behind the curtain speaks of a God who is enthroned in the midst of his people. The altar of incense represents the prayers of God's people, and it represents most dramatically the corporate prayers of God's people.

Individual prayers are important, but there is power in corporate prayer that we are yet to rediscover. As I read the Scriptures, it seems to me that there was an understanding that the burning of incense in God's presence was the most important function performed by the priests.

Going back to that time when Samuel is in the temple, before he begins to function in his ministry, a prophet has come to the old priest, Eli, and spoken to him, rebuking him for his lax parenthood and for his undisciplined sons. God first reminds him of the great privilege he has of being the priest of God:

> *I chose your father out of all the tribes of Israel to be My priest, to go up to My altar, to burn incense, and to wear an ephod in My presence. I also gave your father's house all the offerings made with fire by the Israelites* (1 Samuel 2:28).

God reminds Eli of his high calling: "I chose your fathers. I chose the offspring of your fathers. Now you are in the line of Aaron, and what have I chosen you to do? To go up to my altar and burn incense." It seems as if that was what was recognized as the most important function of the activities in this tabernacle. He did not choose him to make sacrifice, although of course the priest made sacrifice. He did not choose him to go and teach, although teaching was part of the priestly function. He chose him to burn incense. Listen to what Solomon says as he writes to Hiram when he is ready to begin construction on the temple:

> *Now I am about to build a temple for the Name of the Lord my God and to dedicate it to Him for burning fragrant incense before Him* (2 Chronicles 2:4).

Solomon seems to understand that the whole purpose of dedicating this temple is to burn incense to the Lord. It is not one of the most observable things, because it takes place in the holy place and the multitude does not see it happening. Sacrifice takes place in the courtyard. Blood runs deep in the courtyard. Animals are slaughtered in the courtyard. The drama of sacrifice is in the outer precincts. But in the secret place incense continually ascends to the Lord, and that is what he wants. That is what he most desires: a people who are a people of prayer. Hezekiah headed up a revival, and one of manifestations of the revival was the restoration of the house of God. The house of God had fallen into disrepair and disuse. Hezekiah reestablished its function and called again the priests to minister: "*My sons, do not be negligent now, for the Lord has chosen you to stand before Him and serve Him, to minister before Him and to burn incense*" (2 Chron. 29:11).

There seems to be a consensus that the prime ministry is to serve him—to minister before him—and the thing that is highlighted is the burning of incense. The burning of incense is what God was looking for. The burning of incense was what God most desired. God smelled it and was satisfied. God does not lack anything, but I have to speak anthropomorphically because there is no other way we can begin to understand a spiritual God. There is a sense in which we are here to bring satisfaction to the heart of God. Of course, it would be ridiculous and heretical and wrong to suggest that without us there would be dissatisfaction in the heart of God; God is totally self-sufficient, and yet God in his mercy allows us to bring pleasure to Him, allows us to bring satisfaction to His heart. This is epitomized in this whole exercise of burning incense in the presence of God.

The Most Holy Place

The temple was huge, but it was constructed around two rooms of special importance. There was one room, called "the most holy place" or sometimes, in older versions, "the holy of holies." It was a cube. It was the same measurement in length and breadth and height. The only piece of furniture in there was the Ark of the Covenant with the mercy seat upon it, which was overshadowed by two cherubs. It was out of bounds to everybody. In fact, it was only entered once a year on the Day of Atonement by the High Priest. A huge curtain separated it, and on it were embroidered cherubim because the cherubim were the guardians of the presence of God. Just as God had placed cherubim and a flaming sword as guards to keep unregenerate man from going back into the garden and finding the tree of life, so now cherubim guarded the way into God's earthly presence, saying, "You can't come in here." Behind the curtain was the mercy seat and the Ark, God's throne. In fact, God was enthroned in a cloud above the cherubim (see Lev. 16:2; 1 Sam. 4:4). Before this curtain, on the right hand side, was a table with 12 loaves of bread on it; these were called the bread of the presence. This table spoke of a God who was ever present to meet His people's needs. On the left hand side was a seven-pronged lamp. It was fed with oil and kept perpetually burning because it spoke not only of a God who meets His people's needs but of a God who continually speaks to His people.

The Altar and the Ark

All the way back against the curtain was a golden altar of incense that again was tended to on a daily basis to keep it burning. It was a burning altar. It had live coals and incense on it. It was on one side of the curtain, and on the other side of the curtain was the Ark. Let us listen first of all to what Solomon did as he built the sanctuary for God.

> *He partitioned off twenty cubits at the rear of the temple with cedar boards from floor to ceiling to form within the temple an inner sanctuary, the Most Holy Place* (1 Kings 6:16).

And it is this place he is talking about here:

> *So he overlaid the whole interior with gold. He also overlaid with gold the altar that belonged to the inner sanctuary* (1 Kings 6:22).

Here is an interesting statement. It says the altar belonged to the inner sanctuary, but it was actually in the outer sanctuary. It belonged to the Ark, but it was separated from the Ark by a curtain, on which cherubim were embroidered. Why is that? You see, God's purpose was that God and man should be in perpetual intimacy. But sin had separated us from God, and the great curtain was a representation of the barrier that exists between fallen humanity and a holy God. Although this incense altar actually belonged in the inner sanctuary, it had to stay in the outer sanctuary because there was a curtain of separation. That is why when Jesus died on the cross, the curtain of the temple was torn from top to bottom. God was saying, "You can come in now!" The barrier has been removed. In fact, the barrier has not been removed, it has been replaced because we come through a new veil, which is His body. But even back here, they understood that the incense altar actually belonged in the inner sanctuary although it was placed and ministered to in the outer sanctuary.

Now let me take you to Hebrews:

> *Now the first covenant had regulations for worship and also an earthly sanctuary. A tabernacle was set up. In its first room were the lampstand, the table and the consecrated bread; this was called the Holy Place. Behind the second curtain was a room called the Most Holy Place, which had the golden altar of incense and the gold-covered Ark of the Covenant* (Hebrews 9:1-4).

What a surprise! Have we found an error in the Scriptures? No. You see, although this is not a right description, it is a true description. The writer to the Hebrews is conveying to us how it was always intended to be, that the Ark and the altar actually belonged together. It was almost, and I can put it like this, still staying somewhat spiritual, although being very natural, it was like your favorite chair and your footstool. They belong together. You come home. You relax in your favorite chair, but there is something not quite right. Oh dear. The footstool is over the other side of the room, and you are not going to get into total comfort, you are not going to feel totally at peace, until that footstool is in right relationship with your chair, because the two are one in your appreciation. Now in a sense that is true with God. The Ark is His throne upon which He sits, but it is not complete until the footstool altar is in close proximity so that God can enjoy his rest. Now that is how it was supposed to be. When we go into Heaven with John and he gives us a tour of what is going on and he describes what is happening, the two pieces of furniture that are always there are the throne and the altar. In fact, the altar is inevitably described as "the altar that is before the throne" because they are of a piece. They belong together. They are matching furniture, for this throne was overlaid with gold, and so was the altar. They match. They are suited. They belong together. It is the golden altar that is before the throne, and it is the intimacy of God and His people that makes things happen in the Book of Revelation. When we come here, we discover a divine catalyst. It is at this altar, by the way, that Isaiah finds his recommissioning in the purposes of God.

> *In the year that King Uzziah died, I saw the Lord seated on a throne, high and exalted, and the train of His robe filled the temple* (Isaiah 6:1).

I do not know if he was actually in the temple or if he was in vision, but he saw the Lord on His throne. He saw the Ark of the Covenant and the God who is enthroned in the cloud above it, and he saw those seraphim that guard it, crying, "Holy, holy, holy!" and as he saw it, he was overawed with his own sin. It was then that one of the angels came with a live coal from the altar; that is, from the incense altar. He touched his lips. You can escape from things that defile by giving yourself to praise and worship. You can be cleansed in an atmosphere of worship. God sends an angel and makes him whole.

The Significance of the Altar

Luke tells us that Zechariah, the old priest, had gone into the temple to burn incense. It was the time of prayer, and the congregation was outside praying. As he was in the midst of offering up the incense to God, an angel appeared and announced that his prayers had been answered and that God was going to move in his world. He would give him a son who would go before the Lord in the spirit and power of Elijah and make ready a people for the coming of the Lord, and then Messiah would arrive. There is revelation at the incense altar. When Isaiah had been in the presence of the incense altar, his lips got cleaned up. Zechariah's mouth got closed. Through his unbelief he could not speak, but when he did speak, he did not just speak, he prophesied the word of the Lord. This altar is a place of divine encounter.

It is an important place. In fact, Korah's rebellion revolved around this issue. He said, in effect, "Who do you think you are, Moses? Who do you think you are, Aaron? We are all holy. We can all go and offer incense to God." And God said, "Oh no you can't. This is a very important issue. This is the very center of temple worship. You cannot come in when you think you will. You cannot come in because you think you are worthy. You cannot come in unless God draws you in, and in fact you are so badly wrong that the ground is going to open and swallow you up." Korah was sent living down into hell because he presumed that he could come and function in this most holy of ministries. This is also where Uzziah was struck with leprosy: although he was a king, and a good king, and although he had achieved much in the nation and caused it to prosper and brought in peace, he had an ambition to do more. He wanted to burn incense before God because somehow in his understanding that was the most important thing you could do, to come into the presence and burn incense. But the priests withstood him, and even as he stood there railing against the priests, leprosy broke out on his forehead.

The Power of the Altar

The incense altar seems to be quite important! When we read about this, we see the creatures and the elders worshiping God:

> *And when he had taken it, the four living creatures and the twenty-four elders fell down before the Lamb. Each one had a harp and they were holding golden bowls full of incense, which are the prayers of the saints* (Revelation 5:8).

The incense is the prayers of the saints. The psalmist says, "*May my prayer be set before You like incense*" (Ps. 141:2). It has to do with prayer. It is not just to do with saying prayers. It is to do with praying in the Spirit. It is to do with praying in the will of God. It is the prayer that God desires for us to bring him. In Revelation we see how God's throne comes down to earth. One of the ways God's throne comes down into our world is that we pray it down. Jesus said, "*This, then, is how you should pray:... Your Kingdom come*" (Matt. 6:9-10), and we pray down God's throne. Look at how it is described here:

> *Another angel, who had a golden censer, came and stood at the altar. He was given much incense to offer, with the prayers of all the saints, on the golden altar before the throne. The smoke of the incense, together with the prayers of the saints, went up before God from the angel's hand. Then the angel took the censer, filled it with fire from the altar, and hurled it on the earth; and there came peals of thunder, rumblings, flashes of lightning and an earthquake* (Revelation 8:3-5).

You see what is happening. When our prayers touch the throne, the throne touches our world. Our praying brings in the Kingdom. We had better learn how to pray! We had better learn to mean business in prayer. The Book of Revelation teaches us that a praying church brings in God's Kingdom; it shakes our world. Let me just give you a very simple example. They were preaching the name of Jesus. There were signs and wonders, gifts of the Holy Spirit operating, and remarkable miracles taking place. And the religious leaders were offended. The religious leaders were threatened. They took the apostles, and they said, "No more preaching in the name of Jesus. If you preach any more in the name of Jesus, you are in trouble." So they returned to their own people, and they prayed. They lifted up their voices with one accord, and they called on God, and they said, "God, You have seen their threats, you have heard what they have said. Now give us boldness. That is what we need. We need boldness" (see Acts 4:29). This is strange. What they wanted was more of what they already had. When Peter and John had been before the Jewish leaders, the leaders had noticed their boldness (see Acts 4:13). You know that you only get from God what you have already gotten. "*Whoever has will be given more*" (Matt. 13:12). They had *some* boldness, but they wanted *all* boldness. And when they had finished praying, the place where they were praying was shaken. What had happened was that their prayer had touched Heaven, and now Heaven had touched the earth, and it shook. It shook the place where they were. Do you want your town shaken? Get praying.

Paul and Silas were in prison. But instead of complaining, they were singing hymns and praying, and as they prayed there was an earthquake. The place where they were was shaken, and all the doors flew open, and all the chains fell off, and the jailer himself was the first convert for the Kingdom, he and his house. If you want your circumstances to change, start praying. If you want where you are to be shaken, let us learn to pray the prayers that God would have us pray. We have all, I'm sure, been in those prayer meetings of the past, where it was around the world in 30 minutes but nothing really ever happened. It is time for us to learn how to pray. The high priest went into the Most Holy Place to the throne of God once a year, and on the Day of Atonement, it tells us, God said, "I appear in the cloud over the atonement cover," so that when the priest came in, he had to bring his bowl of incense so that the smoke from the incense would rise and conceal the atonement cover so that he would not die as a result of seeing God. I do not know—I am speculating here again, and it may be just mystical—but is it possible that as he went in with the smoke, the smoke of the prayers of the saints mingled with the cloud that was God's presence and there was an intimate merging between God and men that is almost impossible to imagine? He that is enthroned between the cherubim (see Ps. 80:1, etc.) is also enthroned on the praises of Israel (see Ps. 22:3).

How to Pray

Here is how to pray—one simple hint. The incense alter teaches us how to pray. It tells us first of all that there were live coals on the altar, so prayers must be *fervent*. We need prayers from people who have got fire in their bellies. Our prayers must be fervent. It is the fervent prayer of a righteous man that avails much. If you are really requesting, do it with passion. This altar was on fire all the time. Do not pray wet prayers. Do not pray wimpy prayers. Pray with fire. Prayer must be fervent.

Prayer must be *fragrant,* because it was the aroma that went up before God. What I mean by that is simply that our prayers should smell like Jesus. That is, we should pray prayers that Jesus wants us to pray. If you get your prayers from God, then you get them answered. We are an aroma to God. Did you know that? When we get out in the world, some people are attracted by it, and some people are nauseated by it. It is a bit like perfume. Some people think it smells good, and others gag on it! We are like that. To some we are the smell of life and to others the stench of death, but to God we always smell like Jesus, and our prayers should be like that. Pray prayers that God wants to answer. Get your prayers from God and then take them to God. Pray prayers that are full of desire to glorify Jesus.

Finally, our prayers should be *fluent.* I do not mean Shakespearean or in King James English or dramatic and rhetorical, but I mean that they should all flow the same way. In fact, when we find prayers in the New Testament, they all focused on one issue. It is not everything you can think of to fill up the hour of prayer. It is having one issue. For example, if Peter is in prison, what shall we do? We will pray for him to get out of prison. Can we just say a prayer for Auntie Mary because her bunions are acting up? No! We are here to pray for Peter to get out of prison. Prayers are to be disciplined and focused and fluent so that they flow together to achieve the purposes of God.

CHAPTER 2

A Prophetic People

One of the reasons that John's first task was to measure the altar where the worshipers were gathered was because true prayer is very much like prophecy. In fact, when we pray the prayers that God gives us, we are actually prophesying back to God. When Ezekiel found himself in the Valley of Dry Bones, he did not just prophesy to the bones, he prophesied to the Spirit. There is a sense in which when we pray we are speaking God's word back to Him.

Abraham the Prophet

In fact, the first time the word "prophet" is used in Scripture, it is to describe the ministry of Abraham. That should not surprise us because many things begin with Abraham. It is at the time when Abimelech has taken Abraham's wife and God has smitten the whole of Abimelech's household with barrenness. God says, "*Now return the man's wife, for he is a prophet, and he will pray for you*" (Gen. 20:7). So his prophetic ministry was functioning in his prayers. Prayer and prophecy are therefore related. That is why Paul teaches us in Corinthians that when a woman prays or prophesies she does so with her head covered (and a man with his head uncovered). She is ministering as a priest in the purposes of God. Praying and prophesying are sides of the same coin. When I prophesy, I come from the presence of God to you to bring you His word. When I pray, I go into the presence of God from you to take your burdens to Him. To find God recommissioning John into his prophetic ministry and seeing his first task as separating out those who pray at the altar should not surprise us at all. Our first responsibility is to be in the presence of God. In fact, if we do not spend time in the presence of God, we will never hear what God wants to say to us.

Jeremiah was the true prophet of God, but the nation was filled with many false prophets. God said of them that "if they had stood in my council, they would have proclaimed my words" (see Jer. 23:22). What made them false prophets was that they prophesied out of their imagination, and they had not spent time in the presence of God. The mere fact that the incense altar is before the throne actually demonstrates to us where our priority position has to be. We are a people who know what it is to stand before the throne. We bring our prayer, we bring our praise, and we bring our worship, but we also tune our ear to hear what God has to say, and we take the word of God back into our world and our society to mold it accordingly.

Moses the Prophet

It has always been God's desire to fulfill his purpose through a prophetic people. The Bible tells us that when God brought Israel out of Egypt it was by a prophet that he delivered him and by a prophet that he kept him (see Hos. 12:13). Moses the great prophet was God's deliverer. Moses was under tremendous pressure to maintain the equilibrium of the people and motivate them on their pilgrimage. He came to God and he said, "God, it is too much for me. I cannot do it on my own." God said, "Come into the tent of meeting and bring 70 elders with you. I will come down in the cloud and speak to you and I will take the Spirit who is on you and I will put him on them" (see Num. 11:10-17).

One of the things about the prophetic spirit and one of the reasons why we need to recognize and receive a prophet in the name of a prophet is because he carries an anointing that is highly contagious. If you receive him in the right way, his anointing will touch you. So God is going to take the Spirit who is on Moses and puts him on the elders. Moses called the 70 elders. Sixty-eight of them arrived in time for the meeting. This shows us that after thousands of years nothing has changed! But here is what God does. God puts the Spirit not only on the 68 elders in the tent but on the two who are still in the camp.

God demonstrates to us that prophecy is not just for the sanctuary, it is for the street. It is not just for the meeting place, it is for the marketplace. God wants his prophetic word out in the world. But someone was offended that two elders were exercising spiritual functions outside of the sanctuary and ran and reported it. Moses' response was, "*Are you jealous for my sake? I wish that all the Lord's people were prophets and that the Lord would put His Spirit on them!*" (Num. 11:29). That was the desire of Moses. Not just a wishful thought, not just a throwaway line. He was in the presence of God. He was in the cloud. The glory of God was surrounding him, and he is declaring the very heart of God. God wants a prophetic people.

Jesus the Prophet

What Moses desired, Joel centuries later declared had come to pass: in the last days "*I will pour out My Spirit on all people. Your sons and daughters will prophesy*" (Joel 2:28). God is going to have a prophetic community, and what Moses desired and Joel declared, the Day of Pentecost delivered. The church was born as a community of prophets: "*This is what was spoken by the prophet Joel: 'In the last days, God says, I will pour out My Spirit on all people. Your sons and daughters will prophesy, your young men will see visions, your old men will dream dreams'*" (Acts 2:16-17). God has always wanted a prophetic people. The clue to this is that God's ultimate purpose is for us to be like Jesus. So what is Jesus like? If we are going to be like Him, it would be nice to know what He is like.

Well, there are many descriptions. We have seen some dramatic and awesome descriptions of Jesus in the Book of Revelation, and there are many titles of Jesus throughout the Scriptures. In fact, I have got a very thick book that tries to catalog all the names and the titles of Jesus, and given time you could probably think of many names that would stir or comfort us. But you probably would not come up with this one: *prophet.* It does not carry the same emotion, and yet that is what Jesus was. Moses said, "*The Lord your God will raise up for you a prophet like me*" (Deut. 18:15). So if Jesus is the prophet, it follows that if we are to be like Jesus, then we are to be a prophetic people. We belong to a prophetic redeemer.

Elijah the Prophet

Not only was Moses an outstanding prophet and Jesus a prophet like Moses, but the Scripture speaks to us of a more mysterious man who is used as a prophetic paradigm—Elijah. Most prophets in Scripture are introduced as descendents of at least a couple of generations to establish their pedigree. Elijah, however, just turns up. He seems to come from nowhere. In fact, he is described only as "the Tishbite," and nobody really knows where that is or what it means. It means something like "from the settlers among the settlers or among the people who live somewhere," but it is hard for them the biblical writers to describe exactly what it means. But he is a prophet of God, and the Bible has an interesting way of joining these two men, Moses and Elijah, together. In fact, the last chapter of the Old Testament, before the page closes and 400 years of prophetic silence ensue, God speaks and makes a promise.

He says two things. First of all, "*Remember the law of My servant Moses,*" and then, "*I will send you the prophet Elijah before that great and dreadful day of the Lord comes*" (Mal. 4:4-5). These two men are joined together in a sense of expectation. What is more, the sense of expectation is set in the new day that is going to break out in the world. For this chapter begins like this: "*For you who revere My name, the sun of righteousness will rise with healing in its wings*" (Mal. 4:2). Malachi is saying, "There is a new day coming. There is a new sunrise coming, and healing is in its wings, and in that day you will remember my servant Moses, and I will send you Elijah the prophet." So unsurprisingly, when Jesus takes Peter, James, and John up onto the mountain and He prays, His face starts shining like the sun, and His clothes become brilliant white, and there appear with him on the mountain in the glory of his sunshiny face Moses and Elijah (see Matt. 17:1-3). They have turned up in a foretaste of the new day that is about to break.

The Two Witnesses

Revelation chapters 10 and 11 are of one piece. Chapter 10 is the commissioning of a new prophetic thrust, and chapter 11 is the recording of how that prophetic ministry works out. I am sure you are familiar with the two witnesses of whom God speaks. And as you look at these two witnesses, and as you take note of the miracles they perform, you discover that they are identical to the miracles that Moses and Elijah performed. Who the witnesses are we will try to discover, but whoever they are, we already see that their work is characterized by the works of Moses and Elijah. They have been commissioned in John's commissioning by an angel who has a sunshiny face. God's new day has arrived, and God's new day is going to be hallmarked by prophetic anointing and by prophetic ministry.

God has always wanted and always planned for a prophetic people, and the coming of Jesus into the world was the means of achieving it. Down through history he has had prophets. God is not looking for superstars. He is not looking for great platform fame. God is looking for a prophetic people: "*Would that all the Lord's people were prophets and that He would put His Spirit on them!"*

God declares, "*I will give power to My two witnesses, and they will prophesy for 1,260 days*" (Rev. 11:3). In the next three chapters, we are going to find these strange numbers repeated: 42 months; 1,260 days; and "time, times and half a time." You do not need to make too much of that. It is the period in which Elijah shut the heavens so that there would be no rain. It is the length of time that Jesus took to fulfill his earthly ministry. So, in a sense, it represents to us the whole church age, the whole age in which the church is ministering in the name of Jesus, in which we are supposed to demonstrate our power and authority, and in which we are supposed to move in signs and wonders—to reproduce, if you like, the ministry of Elijah in our world.

When Jesus was with the disciples on the mountain, the disciples asked him, "Why do the teachers of the Law say that Elijah must come first?" The teachers of the Law taught that, because that is what the Bible says, as we have already noted: "*I will send you the prophet Elijah*" (Mal. 4:5). Then Jesus replied to his disciples: "*To be sure, Elijah comes and will restore all things.*" But he also told them that "*Elijah has already come,*" and they realized he was referring to John the Baptist (see Matt. 17:9-13).

So we have this enigma, and the enigma of Elijah is the same as the enigma we have with the Kingdom. The Kingdom has come, the Kingdom is coming, and the Kingdom will come. It is not here in fullness, but we have experienced it already. We have tasted the power of the age to come. We are citizens of the Kingdom although the Kingdom is not yet here in all its fullness; that is why we still pray, "Your Kingdom come." But every time there is a sign, a wonder, or a miracle, the Kingdom has advanced. For Jesus said, "*If I drive out demons by the finger of God, then the Kingdom of God has come to you*" (Luke 11:20). That is why we go and preach the Kingdom. We do not preach the Church. We preach the Kingdom. When you preach the Kingdom, Jesus builds the church. His job is to build the Church, and here is a little secret: He is better at it than we are! So, we bring in the Kingdom. Jesus said "*From the days of John the Baptist until now, the Kingdom of Heaven has been forcefully advancing, and forceful men lay hold of it*" (Matt. 11:12). This is what you do: you reach into your tomorrow and you drag it into your today.

Now John, of course, is described as someone who will go before the Lord in the power and spirit of Elijah. The interesting thing about Moses and Elijah is this. They have great similarities. Both of them stood against powerful and hostile kings; they both represented God in moments of intense darkness. Moses stood before Pharaoh when God's people in Egypt were enslaved under political dominion; Elijah stood before Ahab when God's people in Israel were enslaved by spiritual deception and held in demonic darkness. Both had to withstand principalities and powers. Moses had to tackle the magicians of Egypt; Elijah had to tackle the priests of Baal. There was conflict going on; there was warfare. Elijah and Moses represent the two great miracle ages of Israel's history.

When Elisha asked Elijah for a double portion, he was asking to be the eldest son who has the responsibility to carry on the work of the father. There were always miracles among God's people, but these two periods were generational miracle ages. The nation of Israel, when it came out of Egypt, saw God's hand work miracles, signs, and wonders. But when the Israelites came out of Egypt and into the wilderness, they experienced miracles every day for 40 years. It is fantastic to read the accounts. It is exciting. It is also very sobering that although they saw miracles every day for 40 years, they all died in the wilderness, in unbelief. Elijah and Elisha's ministry was the other great miracle age—signs and wonders, miracles of provision, miracles of healing, miracles of resurrection, all kinds of miracles happening on every hand. These two great men represented the dynamic of God, the anointing of God, let loose in their world. They were catalysts of God's power.

Both of them, although not without difficulty, convinced the majority; both of them were able to influence their society. Moses, even with a grumbling and rebellious people, was able to bring them out of Egypt and take them through the wilderness. Elijah was able to turn the hearts of the people back to God. Having seen them limping between two opinions, he focused their hearts and turned them back to the Lord. A whole nation was affected by the ministry of these two men.

Both of them overcame their own weaknesses. One of the things I like about the Scriptures is that God shows us that he uses very real and very ordinary people. Moses, who claimed he could not speak, who said it was too hard, too difficult, too heavy, overcame his own weakness and found his strength in God. Elijah, who was ready to give up, who wanted to lay it all down, who wanted just to lie down and die, overcomes his own weakness, his own burnout, and is ready, in his second spiritual breath, to pursue the purposes of God. If we are going to be God's prophetic people, we are going to have to overcome our own weaknesses. You do not get disqualified for being weak. You do not get disqualified for having weaknesses. But you do disqualify yourself if you do not overcome them.

Both of them were concerned not with their own ministry, but with God's glory. In the case of Moses, God said, "I have had it with this people. I am wiping them out." Moses interceded, "O God, do not do that, your glory is at stake here. If you do that, the other nations will say, 'Ha! He brought them out but he could not bring them in.'" (see Num. 14:11-25). He says, "God, it is your glory at stake." He was concerned for God's glory. Elijah stands before God and says, *"I have been very zealous for the Lord God Almighty"* (1 Kings 19:10). These were people who were sold out for the purposes of God. It is that kind of people who are going to change the world. It is that kind of people who are going to bring in the Kingdom. It is that kind of people whom Jesus is seeking to produce among the churches to whom he is writing in the Book of Revelation. He wants them to understand that it does not matter how weak they are, or how much they have disqualified themselves. He is saying to them, "I can use you. You can be an overcomer. You can be part of the prophetic company that will change the world."

Because we are shown two witnesses here, and because their miracles are so akin to the miracles of Moses and Elijah, many commentators tell us that these two are Moses and Elijah come back again. Others say it is Enoch and Elijah because they are the two men who did not die; they point out that these witnesses are going to be killed, and men have to die once, so it must be those two. I think there is a far simpler and less complex answer to this. God says, "My two witnesses." That is a technical term as far as Scripture is concerned: by the mouth of two or three witnesses every word is established. You can trace that truth from the law of Moses right up to the Book of Revelation (see Deut. 19:15). Jesus himself said, "*In your own Law it is written that the testimony of two men is valid*" (John 8:17). Paul writes to the Corinthians, "*This will be my third visit to you. 'Every matter must be established by the testimony of two or three witnesses'*" (2 Cor. 13:1). Two or three is the number of confirmed witness. It is the number of confirmed truth: "*Do not entertain an accusation against an elder unless it is brought by two or three witnesses*" (1 Tim. 5:19). It is a legal and spiritual requirement with God. So God is not necessarily looking for two individuals, but he is looking for two confessions. He is looking for two words that confirm everything he is doing. He is looking for a corporate witness.

Olive Trees

Now the image here is an interesting and composite one. The witnesses are two olive trees, and they are two lamp stands. Now we have already met lamp stands, and remember the Bible is its own best commentary. Where did we meet lamp stands? It was way back in chapter 1: the seven lamp stands are the seven churches. So lamp stands are churches. And just as seven was the completeness of the church at worship, two is the completeness of the church in its witness, the basic requirement of a confirmed truth. So, we are not seeing individuals, we are seeing the church again in a different function and a different ministry. It is not standing around the throne worshiping; it is out in the world witnessing. That is what they are there for. That is what they are doing. They are God's two witnesses.

Now the olive tree image we first meet, as we have already seen, is found in the prophecy of Zechariah. And it is one of the visions that the angel has to wake him up to see. It is a complicated vision, and we have already said that ultimately the word was this: *"'Not by might nor by power, but by My Spirit,' says the Lord"* (Zech. 4:6). When the prophet asks, "Who are these two olive trees?" they are described as the "sons of oil." I like that. "The sons of oil" or, in another translation, "these are the two anointed ones." But whom do they represent?

When we go back into the Old Testament, we find that consistently there are two categories of people who are anointed, physically anointed with oil tipped over their heads as a symbolic gesture of them receiving the Holy Spirit to function in their ministry. These two categories of people, the two anointed ones, were kings and priests; these were always anointed when they came into their ministry. The problem with that is that when we come into the New Testament, there are no more kings or priests. Or are there? Revelation tells us that we are all priests and kings and we shall rule on the earth: "*You have made them to be a Kingdom and priests to serve our God, and they will reign on the earth*" (Rev. 5:10). We are kings and priests. So who are the two anointed ones? We are! We are the two olive trees. We are the lamp stands. We are the witnesses. We are here to bring his word to our world. This is a picture of the church. It is all the church.

In the eleventh chapter of Romans, Paul tells us that unbelieving Israel, like dead branches, has been cut out of the olive tree. The olive tree is not Israel. The olive tree is God and His purposes. It is Jesus and His power. Israel was a demonstration of what Paul calls the rich sap and root of that olive, because all things are rooted in Christ. Israel only ever succeeded when it recognized it was rooted in Christ. Do you remember how Jesus describes himself in the Book of Revelation? *"I am the Root and the Offspring of David"* (Rev. 22:16). The only reason David could bring forth Jesus was because he was rooted in Jesus. The only way we can bring forth Christ is to be rooted in Christ. So Israel initially was rooted in Christ, and it produced fruit for a short time, for a fleeting season. But when it stopped producing fruit, the branches were cut and cast aside. Some branches remain. Some fruitful branches are a remnant. But God took branches from a wild olive—Gentiles, pagans, heathens—redeemed them by the blood of Jesus, and grafted them into the olive tree so that they became partakers of the same rich sap and root.

Now we can see that these olive branches in Revelation that supply the oil that keeps the church witnessing are Jews and Gentiles. It is the whole people of God. It is people from the East and people from the West, people from the North and people from the South. It is the whole multicolored race of believers who are one holy olive tree in Christ, who produce rich fruit and from whom flows the golden oil. It is Jews and Gentiles, priests and kings. It is also the Law and the Prophets. That is, it is the fullness of the Word, because we can only flow in the Holy Ghost when we are full of the Word. Moses represents the Law and Elijah represents the prophets, so we are to be full of the Word. It is men and women, for *"your sons and daughters will prophesy"* (Joel 2:28).

This is a picture of the Church, the worldwide universal Church of Jesus Christ pursuing its prophetic ministry. They are going to prophesy for 1,260 days while the temple is being trampled for 42 months. It is the same period of course, except months are governed by the moon, which is responsible for the night, and days are governed by the sun, which is responsible for the light (see Gen. 1:16). And things go on simultaneously in our world—for some it is in the day, and for some it is in the night. Everything that happens for us is in the day.

If you noticed in these next three chapters, when John moves from days to months, the days always are to do with God's redeemed people, and the nights are always to do with periods of darkness. It is the same period of time, but it is experienced differently by different people. It is like Israel in Egypt—when God brought great darkness on the land, the sun still shone in Goshen. While our world is in darkness, we are in the light. And we are prophesying, we are speaking God's Word of light into our darkened world.

The Beast from the Abyss

But the world does not like it, and suddenly we are introduced to a character we did not know was coming. When we sat down before this drama began to unfold, took our seats to watch the stage, occupied our important front row seats, and, before the curtain went up and the cast assembled on stage, read down through the list of players, this character was not there. But now abruptly he has turned up—and he is called "the beast from the abyss." Where did he come from? We get no introduction, no explanation. Its simply states, "*Now when they have finished their testimony, the beast that comes up from the*

Abyss will attack them, and overpower and kill them" (Rev. 11:7). There are two very important things to notice here. He could not touch them until they had finished their testimony. Whoever he is, he cannot touch you until you have finished all the ministry that Jesus has entrusted to you. You are invulnerable until you have finished. That is why it is a good idea always to ask Jesus for more to do! When the two witnesses finished their work, he attacked, overcame, and killed them.

We will discover that chapter 13 actually runs parallel to this, and it is in chapter 13 that we get the clue to who this beast is. But I want you to notice that although he attacks, overpowers, and kills them, he has no authority over them. We have looked and seen that when the plagues and horrors are released on our world, they do not come our way, and yet it would be impossible for us to live in a world that was suffering those things and not be affected by them. Some of the spillover will touch us. If a plague comes, we could be infected. I am just using human expressions now. If economic crisis hits a nation, we would be affected. We could not go down to the mortgage society and say, "Excuse me. This does not apply to me. I am a believer. I belong to Jesus." They would not be impressed.

We will be affected by things that touch the world. But we will overcome. We are troubled by the plague, but we believe in a God who heals. We are affected by an economic crisis, but we believe in a God who supplies all our needs. We will have miraculous moments when persecution comes, although we will be touched, and some may die. And I am not looking only at some future time, because persecution is in our world now. There are brothers and sisters of ours today who are laying down their lives for Jesus. There are martyrs being added to that number under the altar daily. In fact, there are more people dying for Jesus now than there probably have been in the history of the church. So when I say "when persecution comes," I am not saying "when this book gets fulfilled, when the West starts seeing the fulfillment of all this book speaks of," because what this book has spoken of is happening already. We could go to nations where the beast is exercising his power. Some will die, inevitably, but we are just walking the path of Jesus. "*For to me, to live is Christ and to die is gain*" (Phil. 1:21).

Paul had a dilemma. It is the only dilemma in the whole of Scripture that I find Paul facing. He did not know what to do—whether to die and be with the Lord or to stay and help his fellow Christians (see Phil. 1:21-26). He said that actually to go and be with the Lord would be far better, but they still needed him, so he would stay. A nice dilemma to have. But the beast from the abyss kills the witnesses, and their bodies lie in the street for three and a half days. John describes the location of their martyrdom as the great city—always a description of Babylon in Revelation, and of Sodom, Egypt, and Jerusalem, the place where their Lord was crucified and which, Jesus said, was the place of every prophetic murder (see Luke 13:33).

These four locations are used to communicate spiritual truths. The witnesses have resisted the seductive deceptions of Babylon. They were not defiled by the sexual deviance of Sodom, nor did they give way to the slavish despair of Egypt, and grace has saved them from the subjecting demands of Jerusalem's religious legalism. John uses the three and a half days as a device because it matches the three and half years, the 42 months and the 1,260 days, and it is also closely related to the time that Jesus was in the tomb. He uses it as a device to explain to us that there is persecution of God's people all the way down through the church age, but just as their Lord was three days in the tomb and rose again, our confidence is that though they slay us yet we will live! They are raised after three and a half days, and they go up to Heaven in a cloud just as their Lord ascended.

We are going to see this repeated in chapter 12. It is the same picture from a different perspective. It says this: "*After the three and a half days a breath of life from God entered them, and they stood on their feet*" (Rev. 11:3). Do you know that is almost identical to the way the resurrection of the dead bones in Ezekiel is recorded? "*Breath entered them,*" says Ezekiel; "*they came to life and stood up on their feet.*" And he adds this: "*a vast army*" (Ezek. 37:10). Every time they kill a servant of God, a vast army arises in his place. The old church fathers used to say, "The blood of the martyrs is the seed of the church." It was as if every drop that was shed was the fertilizer that brought forth new life. Do you remember how Jesus described his own death? He says, "*I tell you the truth, unless a kernel of wheat falls to the ground and dies, it remains only a single seed. But if it dies, it produces many seeds*" (John 12:24).

One death, multitudes of life. Look at the harvest that has come from the laying down of the life of the Lord Jesus, and look at the harvest in many parts of our world where the martyred church is growing in remarkable ways. O you foolish devil! O you crazy demons! Don't you know that every time you martyr the servants of God, God causes a multitude to rise? Don't you know?

> *We do, however, speak a message of wisdom among the mature, but not the wisdom of this age or of the rulers of this age, who are coming to nothing. No, we speak of God's secret wisdom, a wisdom that has been hidden and that God destined for our glory before time began. None of the rulers of this age understood it, for if they had, they would not have crucified the Lord of glory* (1 Corinthians 2:6-8).

If satan had understood the wisdom of God! If the rulers and the principalities had understood the wisdom of God! Satan does not know everything. Satan only reacts against what God initiates. He is not all-knowing.

Some Christians in this age have the misconception that there is a battle going on between equal powers. In fact, the way some of them preach and teach and live, you would think satan is more powerful. They certainly think a curse has greater power than the blessing of God. There are people walking around believing they have curse on them. Listen! You have been blessed in Jesus, and if you are blessed you cannot be cursed. They brought on old Balaam and asked him to curse God's people and he replied, "*How can I curse those whom God has not cursed?*" (Num. 23:8). There is no divination against Jacob. There is no curse on you. You live in the blessing of God.

Satan does not know it all. He is not all-powerful. He is not everywhere, either. If satan is hounding you, it means he is leaving me alone, because he cannot be on to both of us at the same time. If they had understood, they would not have crucified the Lord of glory. Well, of course, they would have because there is enmity in their hearts. They cannot do anything else about it. Satan encountered one Jesus, and all his animosity focused on that one Jesus. All his dark machinations were spent against that one Jesus. He saw that one Jesus nailed to a cross. He watched that one Jesus die. He saw that one Jesus buried, and he saw to his horror a multitude of Jesus rising from the dead, witnesses raised up into life because God is with them and God is for them. And God gains a great victory through them, for it tells us that only 7,000 people perished in the earthquake that ensued.

Now that is interesting because when Elijah was before God, there were only 7,000 who were true to the Lord, and the whole nation was in apostasy. Now we discover there are only 7,000 who perish—but the vast majority give glory to God. The ministry of the prophetic witness has been effective, and multitudes have been saved. That is God's will and purpose for us.

CHAPTER 3
The Flood from the Abyss

The Book of Revelation not only unveils Christ, it also unmasks the devil. It shows us who he really is. It shows us his devices. The apostle Paul could say to the church that they were not ignorant of satan's devices (see 2 Cor. 2:11). Unfortunately, we could probably not say that about the church today.

We Are in a Battle

We are living in the days when Paul says that there will be those who "*follow deceiving spirits and things taught by demons*" (1 Tim. 4:1). Although we know that Christ is triumphant, that all things are under his feet, and that he has crushed the serpent's head, there is still satanic and demonic activity going on in our world. I say that not to alarm us, but just to make us aware of the kind of world that we live in. We are called to battle, and "*our struggle is not against flesh and blood, but against the rulers, against the authorities, against the powers of this dark world and against the spiritual forces of evil in the heavenly realms*" (Eph. 6:12). Now the outcome of the battle has already been confirmed and established, but it is a battle.

The Book of Judges is a very important book because it instructs us about taking the world for the Kingdom. God called the Israelites to take the land. He calls us to take the world. He promised them that every place that the soles of their feet would tread he would give to them (see Deut. 11:24; Josh. 1:3). A promise like that could make them believe that the taking of the land would literally be a walkover. But it was not. There were battles to win, cities to take, and armies to put to flight. The same thing is true today. It is an unequal battle, of course, and one could almost feel that it is unfair to be part of a side that cannot lose confronting a side that cannot win. But that is how it is, and we should all be glad of it!

The Restless Sea

When you read the Bible you will discover that God seems, at times, to have a problem with the sea, with the oceans. One significant Scripture that underlines that we find towards the end of Revelation, when the perfection of beauty has come, when the city has descended out of Heaven in all its splendor and glory and when God removes the curse from our world. There is a simple statement that tells us "*there was no longer any sea*" (Rev. 21:1). There is a river but no sea. There is no more sea because the sea is often used in Scripture as a picture of that which restlessly resists the will of God. Let us consider some Scriptures to confirm this. Here is God speaking to Job, rebuking him and challenging him as to where he was in the midst of all God's creative activity.

> *Who shut up the sea behind doors when it burst forth from the womb, when I made the clouds its garment and wrapped it in thick darkness, when I fixed limits for it and set its doors and bars in place, when I said, "This far you may come and no farther; here is where your proud waves halt"?* (Job 38:8-11)

God is speaking to a restless ocean that seems to have energy that wants to break the bounds that God has set. And God stands beside the ocean and says, "I have set your doors, I have fixed your bars, I have put limits on you. You can come this far and no further." It is almost as if, at times, the ocean is in antagonism against God. That is why Jesus rebuked the sea and commanded it to be still. He is taking authority over that which, at that particular time, appears to be seeking to destroy him. He demonstrates his authority over the restless sea by walking on it to show that even this great rebellious mass is under His feet, just as the angel set His foot upon the ocean.

Listen to what the writer of Proverbs surprisingly says about this. It is wisdom speaking, saying how she was there at every stage of God's creative power, "*when He gave the sea its boundary so the waters would not overstep His command, and when He marked out the foundations of the earth*" (Prov. 8:29).

God has put a boundary on the oceans. He has put a limit on the activity of the seas.

God speaks through Jeremiah to rebuke his people because they do not submit to His authority or obey His word:

> *I made the sand a boundary for the sea, an everlasting barrier it cannot cross. The waves may roll, but they cannot prevail; they may roar, but they cannot cross it* (Jeremiah 5:22).

There are many other Scriptures that seem to portray this apparent antagonism between God and the ocean, between the Lord and the sea. It is as if the sea is seeking to burst out, to overcome the barrier, to roll, with its waves, across the limits that God has set upon it. There is a fight going on.

We are perhaps given a clue as to why this is when we consider the words of Isaiah:

> *But the wicked are like the tossing sea, which cannot rest, whose waves cast up mire and mud* (Isaiah 57:20).

In Scripture the rebellious nations of the world are often pictured as the sea. That is why the prostitute in the Book of Revelation is described as being seated on many waters. The many waters that she sits upon are peoples and nations and tongues. They are the nations of the world, and they are represented as the many waters that cover the face of our earth.

We can recognize, then, that the sea somehow contains some unpleasant concepts. It is the very place where, when God was looking for somewhere to cast our sin, he threw it. And another name for the sea, or the deep, is the abyss. Abyss is a very interesting word in Revelation. We are dealing with rebellious nations, with the wicked who are like the tossing sea, always wanting to go over the limits, to push back the boundaries of their immorality, wickedness and violence. This is not just an Old Testament concept. Jesus described people approaching the end times:

> *On the earth, nations will be in anguish and perplexity at the roaring and tossing of the sea* (Luke 21:25).

There is a disturbance among the nations. There is a perplexity and confusion, and it is described as the tossing of the sea. Jesus once came to a place where the Gadarenes lived, and He met a man with demons. When Jesus asked the name of the demon, the response was "*Legion, for we are many*" (Mark 5:9). The man was possessed with a legion of demons, and the demons began to implore Jesus that He would not send them back to the abyss. So Jesus cast out the demons from the man into a herd of pigs, and the pigs ran headlong down the slope and drowned in the sea, because that is where all unclean things belong. It is the abode of evil. It is the depository of sin. Fortunately for our world, it is a deep pit that is sealed and locked. Having said that, we need to consider some of the things that come up out of the abyss.

The Beasts

When we were looking at God's prophetic people in chapter 11 of the Book of Revelation, we suddenly had this word dropped on us that seemed to come out of the blue, but it actually came out of the pit. It was the word that told us that the beast from the abyss would fight against God's prophetic people and would kill them. There is no more said about him. It is just like a throwaway line, but then we turn to chapter 13; this is why we cannot see the book chronologically, as this is a flashback to tell us what actually happened.

It was just a single line in chapter 11 that told us that it happened; the whole explanation is given in chapter 13. John says, "*And I saw a beast coming out of the sea*" (Rev. 13:1). This is the beast from the abyss. Now remember that the sea also represents the restless wickedness of Gentile nations, and so the beast that comes up out of the sea is actually a representation of anti-Christian political power. It is bestial in its hatred of the things of God, in its agendas, and in its oppression. In the first century, the beast that came out of the sea was the Roman Empire, and for Israel, of course, it literally came out of the sea: it came from across the ocean.

When we look at the description of this beast, we discover that it is a composite picture of the four beasts that Daniel saw coming up out of the sea. If you refer back to the Book of Daniel, you will find that he saw four beasts coming up out of the ocean. Daniel speaks of four empires yet to come, the last of which will be the most oppressive, the most violent, and the most destructive. He sees first the Babylonian Empire, then the Medo-Persian Empire, the Greek Empire, and finally the Roman Empire.

The Roman Empire was worse than everything that had been before it. When I was at school, we used to get taught about things like the Pax Romana, all the good things that the Romans did, all the rule and peace that they established. But it was a most cruel and oppressive empire, given to violence and bloodshed, and at this time it was epitomized by a hedonistic emperor called Nero. Nero became emperor at the age of 17 and later had his mother murdered. An ex-wife and countless officials were also similarly dispatched. He pursued "sexual activities of great and indeed unlimited versatility" and instituted the youth games that attracted "every sort of immorality" (Tacitus, quoted in Michael Grant, *The Roman Emperors* [New York: Barnes and Noble, 1985]). In A.D. 64 vast tracts of Rome were destroyed by fire, which many believed was ordered by the Emperor himself in order to create space for the building of a huge golden house for the indulgence of his pleasures. He then went on to use the Christian community in Rome as scapegoats for the conflagration.

The historian Seneca recorded, "Dressed in wild animal skins they were torn to pieces by dogs or made into torches to be ignited after dark" (quoted in Grant, op. cit.). This Neronian persecution formed the prototype of others in later reigns. After his death a legend arose that a risen Nero would return, making him a certain candidate for the beast.

One of the great conflicts we have in Revelation is between the beast and the Lamb. Later on, in chapter 13, there is another beast, but he does not come out of the sea; he comes out of the land and represents religious power yoked with political power. When you get religious power and political power together, you have a nightmare scenario. You only have to look at nations whose government is fundamentalist Islam to know that those combinations spell murder. This is true of any coalition of religion and politics.

The antagonism of Rome towards Christianity was provoked by believers' refusal to sacrifice to Caesar. This is a theme all the way down through history: God is at war with the beast from the sea and the beast from the land, with political and religious powers. If you want a little bit of background on the beast from the land and the beast from the sea, read the last two chapters of the Book of Job. Here there are two beasts. There is a land beast called "Behemoth" and a sea beast called "Leviathan." Modern commentators tell us that they are an elephant and a crocodile but, as I read it, I think that I have never seen either an elephant or a crocodile like what is described there! They are actually much more akin to dinosaurs, and one must wonder if the remnants of dinosaurs still walked the earth in the days of Job.

How do these beasts relate to the political and religious powers? Well, consider what the psalmist says in Psalm 74. He is talking about God delivering his people from Egypt and crushing Leviathan, who is identified as Rahab (see Ps. 89), the meaning of which implies "a tempestuous and arrogant attitude." There is a very real sense in which the first political and religious conflict for Israel was in Egypt, because the pressure there was both economic and moral. It was political because Israel was an asset to the Egyptian economy. One of the things that Pharaoh was worried about was that the people were getting so big that they would leave the land, and he did not want them to do that because they were good for his economy. He did not want them to stay, either, because he was afraid they would fight him (see Exod. 1:10).

That is a dilemma that the world always has with the Church. It is the dilemma that, for example, a company may have with its Christian worker. They want him there because he's the best worker in the place. But they do not want him there because he is a provocation to their loose morals. He does not fit in with everybody else, and there is this love/hate relationship. They think, "We don't want to get rid of him because he makes us money; we would like to get rid of him because he embarrasses us." Israel was like that in Egypt. They loved them, and they hated them. They wanted them, and they did not want them. But God delivered them and, according to the psalmist, God delivered them from the beast from the ocean.

> *It was You who split open the sea by Your power; You broke the heads of the monster in the waters. It was You who crushed the heads of Leviathan and gave him as food to the creatures of the desert* (Psalm 74:13-14).

God demonstrates his deliverance of Israel out of Egypt as a crushing of the head of the sea monster.

> *You crushed Rahab like one of the slain; with Your strong arm You scattered Your enemies* (Psalm 89:10).

This is how Isaiah puts it:

> *Was it not You who cut Rahab to pieces, who pierced that monster through? Was it not You who dried up the sea, the waters of the great deep, who made a road in the depths of the sea so that the redeemed might cross over?* (Isaiah 51:9-10)

When He moved in judgment and delivered his people out of Egypt, God crushed the sea monster, Pharaoh, Rahab, in order to bring his people through. He overcame the political oppression, for as slaves they had been vital to the Egyptian economy. He overcame the religious oppression, for He brought judgment not just on Egypt, but on the gods of Egypt (see Exod. 12:12).

There is a war going on, then, but our God gives us victory and brings us through in deliverance. The beast from the abyss might come and roar, but he will be defeated.

True Spiritual Warfare

In order for me to communicate something about what we are facing by way of spiritual warfare, we are going to turn to chapter 9 of the Book of Revelation. Here we begin to get into some of the nightmare scenarios.

> *The fifth angel sounded his trumpet, and I saw a star that had fallen from the sky to the earth* (Revelation 9:1a).

Now that is exactly how the prophets describe the fall of satan (see Isa. 14:12-14). John continues to write:

> *The star was given the key to the shaft of the Abyss* (Revelation 9:1b).

We should note that he does not have the key; he does not possess the key and has no right to the key. He cannot use the key until the key is given to him, because every key that opens every purpose is on Jesus' belt. He has the keys of death and hell. He has the keys of David. Nothing can be unlocked without Jesus' approval. So, then, this angel is given the key to the Abyss.

> *When he opened the Abyss, smoke rose from it like the smoke from a gigantic furnace. The sun and sky were darkened by the smoke from the Abyss. And out of the smoke locusts came down upon the earth and were given power like that of scorpions of the earth. They were told not to harm the grass of the earth or any plant or tree, but only those people who did not have the seal of God on their foreheads. They were not given power to kill them, but only torture them for five months. And the agony they suffered was like that of the sting of a scorpion when it strikes a man. During those days men will seek death,*

> *but will not find it; they will long to die, but death will elude them. The locusts looked like horses prepared for battle. On their heads they wore something like crowns of gold, and their faces resembled human faces. Their hair was like women's hair, and their teeth were like lions' teeth. They had breastplates like breastplates of iron, and the sound of their wings was like the thundering of many horses and chariots rushing into battle. They had tails and stings like scorpions, and in their tails they had power to torment people for five months. They had as king over them the angel of the Abyss, whose name in Hebrew is Abaddon, and in Greek, Apollyon. The first woe is past; two other woes are yet to come* (Revelation 9:2-12).

Now this is the happy hunting ground for the sensational and the bizarre and those who want to interpret the Scripture by the morning's newspaper. The first thing we need to understand about these locusts is that they are not, as some have foolishly suggested, helicopters! They are demons. They have come up out of the Abyss. They have been released, but they have only been released for a short while. Now remember that the sea is the Abyss. They are synonymous. This, then, is a tidal wave of evil breaking out in the world, first fulfilled in the awful things that happened in Jerusalem before it fell. That was its first fulfillment: a tidal wave of evil, sweeping all men before it.

These demons have the ability to torment men for five months. It is interesting that the flood, by which God removed all life from the earth except the life of the eight saved in the Ark, prevailed over the earth for five months. What we are seeing here is a flood of evil that comes into the land and submerges all people for five months. It is another flood. It came from the abyss, just as in Noah's day the fountains of the deep were opened in order to bring the flood upon the ground. Here there is not a literal flood of water but a flood of evil. It flows out of the abyss to cover the land where God's covenant-breaking people are currently abiding.

I do not think for a moment that we are supposed to analyze these creatures too much. I think that the description is just meant to fill us with horror and repulsion. It is so bizarre, so ugly, and so contrary to anything that is pleasant and acceptable that these horrible creatures are supposed simply to fill us with absolute abhorrence. Having said that, I am going to suggest some of the things they could represent.

The image is taken from the prophet Joel. In the first two chapters of Joel, the prophet is speaking about what he calls the army of the Lord, but it is actually an invasion of the land by an unprecedented swarm of locusts. Joel speaks of that as a godly judgment on the nation, and much of Joel's imagery is repeated throughout the Book of Revelation. In fact, things that, in Joel, are regarded as demonstrations of judgment are sometimes taken in the New Testament as pictures of God's blessing, for example, the signs in the sky, blood, vapor of smoke, and signs in the heavens.

In the New Testament, rather than being a sign of utter disaster and total condemnation, these are the signs that accompany the coming of the Holy Spirit and the anointing of the people of God. So signs can be both: to the perishing they are portents of disaster, and to the righteous they are promises of blessing.

Let me just highlight this point again by taking you back to the flood and to Noah. The writer to the Hebrews tells us that Noah, being warned by God of things not yet seen, moved with reverent fear and built an ark for the salvation of his family. The whole purpose of the ark was to save. It had no other purpose. It was the means of God's salvation. Just as baptism is, for us, a demonstration of our salvation, it is also a picture of us going through the flood. The writer to the Hebrews says that the sole reason Noah built the ark was to save, but then he goes on to say that by building the ark, Noah condemned the world (see Heb. 11:7). That was not his aim. His aim was to save, but the by-product was condemnation. So the Ark, which was for Noah and his family a wonderful picture of salvation, was for the unbeliever a sign of condemnation.

Equally, the cross for us is a wonderful sign of redemption; to the world it is the very thing that condemns them. For not only did salvation come into the world by the cross, but Jesus says that now, in other words through his death on the cross, judgment comes into the world. By the cross we are saved, and by the cross the prince of this world is driven out (see John 12:31). So one thing can have radically different effects on different people.

Therefore, we are seeing things that will not harm *us*, things that should not cause us to fear. The whole purpose of locusts is to eat everything green. It eats every leaf, strips every bush bare, and takes the grass away so that a desert is left behind. In fact, the Book of Joel describes it like this: "*Before them the land is like the garden of Eden, behind them, a desert waste—nothing escapes them*" (Joel 2:3). But these locusts do not eat the trees or the grass. Clearly they are not natural locusts but spirit beings who are only fulfilling the purpose of God. In fact, as you read it, you will find that they are restricted in what people they can touch. They can only touch those who do not have the mark of God. That means those who carry the mark of God are untouched in this satanic epidemic. The locusts are restricted as to the people they can affect. They are also restricted in their power: they are not allowed to kill anybody. And they are restricted in the period of their operation: it can only last five months. We need to understand and appreciate that whatever satan seeks to do, whatever demon powers seek to accomplish in our world, they are on a leash that Jesus holds in his hand. There are restrictions on them, like there are on the restless ocean. He says that they are to go "*this far…and no farther*" (Job 38:11).

Let us just have a look at them, not because there is anything desirable about them, but to consider why John describes them as he does. It is possible that he cannot find any other words and he uses the best dynamic equivalent he has got in his language to communicate what his eye sees. But maybe he uses this imagery for a specific purpose.

The first thing that happens when the abyss opens is that there are billows of impenetrably *dark smoke,* so much so, actually, that John describes it as darkening the sun and the sky. That is how the locust swarm is described in the Book of Joel. They come with such density that they block out light. These creatures produce darkness. They produce an atmosphere in which you cannot see, in which you are uncertain and confused. They come to *darken* the minds and the understandings of those who are outside of Christ. They bring confusion into the thinking of men and women. This darkness is the great locust cloud that fills the sky.

But they are also described as those who are like *scorpions*. What is more, these scorpions sting people and torture and torment them to such an extent that men will seek to die, but will not find death as a way out of their torment because these creatures have come to produce *despair* in the hearts of people.

They are then described as *horses*, and horses in the Scriptures were the equivalent of weapons of mass destruction in our day. Israel was forbidden to multiply horses, but powerful nations had horses and chariots. Israel was forbidden to have them because that is what Egypt had. That is what Egypt boasted in, and a nation with horses was a nation that could dominate its neighbors. A nation with horses was a nation with an equipped army that could subdue all those around it. And so these locusts are like horses because they have come to *dominate* the lives of all those to whom they carry their influence and their power.

They are described as having *human faces*. That is because all demon power works through humanity. A human person demonized is the means of mass deception. They perpetuate doctrines of demons that lock people up, that *deceive*, that captivate. I am only speculating, but when we set it in the context of imagery and concepts used throughout Scripture, these are distinct possibilities.

They had *women's hair* because these creatures create carnal *desires* in the hearts of people. A woman's hair is her glory. It is a display of her femininity and a demonstration of her beauty. In the Song of Solomon the king says that the tresses of his lover captivate him. While that is legitimate in true love, it is destructive when it produces lust.

They have got *lion's teeth* because they have come to *devour* everything that is good in the lives of those whom they are seeking to oppress.

In summary, these demons are producing a society that is in the dark, that is in despair, that feels it is being dominated by powers outside of itself, that has been deceived by humanism behind which is demonic powers. They produce a society with inordinate desires to fulfill growing longings and a society that is being devoured, chewed up, and spat out. I sometimes feel that I live in a society just like that, and I find this far scarier than helicopters! I find this more challenging because I cannot do anything to stop the helicopter, but I can seek to change my society.

Do you remember when Jesus sent out the 72, instructing them to heal the sick, cleanse the lepers, preach the good news to the poor, and cast out demons? When they come back, they exclaimed, "*Lord, even the demons submit to us in Your name*" (Luke 10:17). Jesus then declares, "*I saw Satan fall like lightning from Heaven*" (Luke 10:18). They must have thought to themselves, "We didn't see that!" They saw the leper cleansed, but they did not see satan fall. They were looking where the problem and the need were because that was their area of responsibility and ministry. But Jesus saw satan fall out of the sky.

Christians can get into all kinds of things about spiritual warfare and territorial mapping and such. But that is not our responsibility. Our responsibility, our challenge and privilege, is to reach the world. We have to preach the Gospel, heal the sick, and deliver the possessed. I have not got time to deal with satan. But the good news is that when I do my job, he falls out of the sky! I do not have to pull him down. He falls down. We do not need to make a ministry out of something that Jesus has already done. Then Jesus says to them, *"I give you authority over all the power of the enemy to tread on serpents and scorpions"* (Luke 10:19).

Those things just get out of the pit for us to tread on. They are awful, foul, evil, and wicked, and they have come to corrupt our society. It was part of God's judgment on covenant-breaking Israel, but they are still out there. Demon powers are still operating in our world, and our strategy is simple. We preach the Gospel. We cast out demons by the Spirit of God, and then we know that the Kingdom has come.

CHAPTER 4

The Unholy Trinity

We ended the last chapter with the locusts that came up from the abyss. And we saw that we can chase them all the way back down to the pit because they cannot touch us—we have been given authority to tread on snakes and scorpions. It reveals something about them, too, when it tells us that "*on their heads they wore something like crowns of gold*" (Rev. 9:7) and that "*they had breastplates like breastplates of iron*" (Rev. 9:9). If we apply that to the world in which we live, it speaks of people who are impostors, people who are their own kings and who think only of themselves. They do not have real authority. They only have what look like crowns. But it's a pose and a posture. They say, "I am in charge. I am all that matters. I am king of my own life. I am lord of my own destiny. I make my own decisions. I rule." Of course, that is the ultimate rebellion against God.

Not only do they wear things that look like crowns of gold, but they also have iron breastplates. That is, they are untouched and unmoved by anything but their own desires. They have encased their hearts in iron shields. They are indifferent to anybody else, to the needs, desires, or hurts of others. Demons do not just fly around in the air; they come to affect society. We cannot be certain exactly what form and nature this takes, though I have suggested some possibilities. It is important to note that the demon powers are not just floating around in the sky; they are at work now in the sons of disobedience (see Eph. 2:2). That is why, in our preaching of the Gospel, we cast out demons and heal the sick.

As we have been considering the kind of society that demonic activity produces, let me take you back to chapter 11 and show its connection with chapter 13. In chapter 11 we were looking at God's prophetic company. There we had two witnesses, whereas in chapter 13 we have two beasts, one from the sea and one from the land. There are some remarkable contrasts between the two witnesses and the two beasts. I would like to point some out to you. The witnesses are called to prophesy (see Rev. 11:3); the beast is given a mouth to blaspheme (see Rev. 13:5). The witnesses prophesy for 1,260 days (governed by the sun) because they are God's sunshine people; the beast has authority for 42 months (governed by the moon) because he is a worker in the darkness. Fire comes from the mouths of God's prophets (see Rev. 11:5); fire is called down from Heaven by the false prophet (see Rev. 13:13). The beast from the land, by the way, is, after this moment, called the false prophet, and because he calls fire down out of the sky, he is particularly a false Elijah.

The Beast from the Land

The beast from the land, the false prophet, is said to look like a lamb, having two horns. But though he looks like a lamb, he speaks like a dragon. Part of the strategy of the beasts that are against the purposes of God is to deceive us. Jesus said, "*Watch out for false prophets. They come to you in sheep's clothing, but inwardly they are ferocious wolves*" (Matt. 7:15). We must not take anything on face value. We test the spirits to see if they are of God. Paul, in fact, when he is saying farewell to the Ephesian elders, encourages them to remain in the faith and shepherd the flock that God has purchased with his own blood because "*I know that after I leave, savage wolves will come in among you and will not spare the flock*" (Acts 20:29). Then he says, soberly, that some of those wolves will come "*even from your own number*" (Acts 20:30). Now these may not be the ultimate beast described in Revelation, but they are bestial manifestations.

An interesting teaching of the Scriptures is that the further away you get from God, the more bestial you become. The evolutionists will tell us that we started off as animals and evolved into these wonderful creatures that we recognize as human. The Bible tells us that we started off perfect and ended up like animals. It is full of bestial imagery to describe humans apart from God: those that reject the Gospel are like dogs that turn back to their own vomit; those who deny Christ are like pigs that get out of the mire and turn back and wallow in it again (see 2 Pet. 2:22).

We are told in chapter 11 that the beast from the abyss will attack, overpower, and kill the prophets of God (see Rev. 11:7).

In chapter 13 it is restated that the beast is given power (right and might) to make war against the saints and to conquer them (see Rev. 13:7). What we are seeing is the same thing happening but from a different perspective. Here is an another interesting observation: the inhabitants of the earth rejoice over the death of the prophets (see Rev. 11:9), and the whole world follows the beast (see Rev. 13:3). One of the reasons they follow the beast is because the beast has a fatal wound that has been healed (see Rev. 13:3). He has a false resurrection.

What does that mean? Well, this was a dilemma for the early church. They knew that the Son of God was going to bruise the serpent's head. They wrote that Jesus, through His death, would destroy him who had the power of death, the devil. That was their confidence and their expectation. And in the first flush of their excitement as the Gospel spread throughout the whole world, there seemed to be no stopping them.

It seemed as if they would soon fulfill the Great Commission and bring all nations in submission to the Lord, but then came vicious opposition and persecution. Here was the reemergence of terrible evil and wickedness and awful happenings, and perhaps they thought to themselves, "This beast is not dead after all!" The continuance of evil in our world is one of the great arguments people use to deny the truth of the Gospel. But we must recognize that the beast has been defeated. He has been overcome even though his ultimate destruction is yet to come. The purposes of God cannot be held back. We will trample on serpents and scorpions because that is what we are equipped to do.

When the Scripture talks to us about putting on the whole armor of God in the sixth chapter of Ephesians, it describes that armor from the helmet down to the boots, the big hob-nail sandals like the Roman soldiers wore. These boots have a name. Every piece of armor has a name. The helmet is called Salvation, the breastplate is called Righteousness, the belt is Truth, the shield is Faith, the sword is Word of God, and the boots are called Peace. Now that is an odd name for boots in which people are going out to war. You would think the boots would be called War or Conflict or Strife. But these boots are called Peace, because, although we are marching to war, our war song is all about the Prince of Peace.

We win by bringing people into submission to His lordship. That is why, when Paul writes to the Romans, he says, "*The God of peace will soon crush Satan under your feet*" (Rom. 16:20). It is the God of peace whom we follow. You have got boots on that are called Peace and, if you have got ears to hear, listen to the squelching as you walk; you are treading on snakes and scorpions everywhere you go, and you are creating a path of peace.

In chapter 11, after three and a half days, the breath of life from God enters into the two witnesses. But look at this horrific parallel and parody in chapter 13. This is the second beast, the false prophet, who has made an image of the first beast, and we are told that he was given power to give breath to the image of the first beast (see Rev. 13:14-15). Now it is not that he has created some kind of android, an automaton or robot. He is producing a society. When God created man he breathed into him life that the man might become the father of a new society (see Gen. 2:7). When Jesus rose from the dead and met his disciples, he breathed on them and said, "*Receive the Holy Spirit*" (John 20:22) because he was making them into his new redeemed community, a new society in the world. So when the false prophet breathes breath into the image of the beast, he is producing a society that is demonized. Just as the spirit of Jesus makes us like himself, so the breath of the beast makes his followers conform themselves to "*the spirit who is now at work in those who are disobedient*" (Eph. 2:2).

There are only two kinds of people in this world: the redeemed and the lost, those who are in the light and those who are in the dark, those who are in the Kingdom of God and bow to His lordship and those who are in the kingdom of satan and are manipulated by his power. There is a society out there that has been breathed on by evil and is motivated by evil intention. There is another society that has been breathed on by the Spirit of God and is empowered not only to overcome but to transform it into the society of the redeemed. It is the demonic, satanic, sinful society that receives the mark of the beast's ownership upon them. That is where our warfare lies. That is where our conflict is.

There is an unholy trinity in operation: the dragon, the beast from the sea, and the beast from the land known as the false prophet. There is a satanic power that manipulates the political powers of our world, and there is a conniving, religious authority harnessed to that beast in order to pursue all that satan wants to do. Now we have seen already, and we know in our own hearts, that it is an unequal battle, for the Holy Trinity outweighs the unholy trinity infinitely. And yet the war is still being fought. The beast may have overcome the saints and killed them, but we have come to understand that being killed does not mean being defeated.

The Dragon and the Woman

Chapter 12 begins with an incredible vision of a woman in the heavens. Let us note the key thing here. In the second part of this vision, there is, in front of the woman, as she is waiting to give birth, a huge red dragon. The sole intent of this dragon is to devour her child as soon as it is born. Now this image takes us way back in the Bible to the first declaration of the Gospel, to what theologians call the "protoevangelion." The first preaching of the Gospel is actually directed at satan, to whom it is not good news! And it happens in the Garden of Eden after satan has tempted the woman and sin has come into the world.

God says to satan that he is cursed above all the animals, and he says, "*And I will put enmity between thee and the woman, and between thy seed and her seed; it shall bruise thy head, and thou shalt bruise his heel*" (Gen. 3:15 KJV). From that moment on, satan has lived in fear. We find this concept of the devil's fearful reaction to newborn children occurring all the way through Scripture.

That is why, when Moses was about to come into the world, the serpent whispered to the king, "Kill the babies; kill all the babies" and that is what Pharaoh sought to do, because there is always enmity between the serpent and the seed of the woman. He tried to do it when Jesus was born and came into the world. The serpent whispered again, this time to Herod, "Kill all the babies; kill all the babies." Our enemy, Peter warns us, is like a roaring lion that goes around seeking whom he may devour (see 1 Pet. 5:8). He wants to devour the seed of the woman, but God preserves his chosen seed.

This picture in the twelfth chapter of Revelation, then, is the climax, the ultimate picture, of what has been going on down throughout history. There has always been enmity between the serpent and the seed of the woman, but here is the good news: the chosen seed is always preserved. Moses actually enjoys the privilege of growing up in Pharaoh's house. It proves that God is able to keep His own secure.

The Beast from the Abyss

The dragon is poised to devour the seed of the woman and pursues her into the wilderness. This is nothing less than a reenactment of Israel's escape from Egyptian bondage and from Pharaoh, of which more later. The old dragon lurks in the waters, but now the beast from the Abyss is described in this way,

> *The beast I saw resembled a leopard, but had feet like those of a bear and a mouth like that of a lion* (Revelation 13:2).

He is a pretty awesome creature. He looks like a leopard because he is swift. Have you noticed in the Scripture how sinners are often described as those who are swift to shed blood, as those who are in the fast lane of evil? Well this beast is swift to do evil. He has bear's feet because he is strong. Jesus describes satan as the "strong man." He has got a mouth like a lion, as did those demon powers from the pit, which inevitably have some of his characteristics. He has a mouth like a lion because he is savage. It is interesting, by the way, that David, even before he was anointed, before he ever came into his kingdom, killed a lion and a bear. God's people can overcome this beast. And later on he kills a giant, Goliath. If you read the description of Goliath and the bronze armor he wore, and then compare that with Job's description of Leviathan, it looks as if Goliath was a monster. He had that scaly armor just like Leviathan did from head to foot. He seemed invulnerable. He seemed unbeatable. And when God spoke to Job about Leviathan, he said, "What can you do? Can you overcome him? Are you strong enough to handle him? Can you pull him out with a hook?" The clear implication is, "Oh no, you can't. But I can" (see Job 41:1). Our God overcomes all the beasts, all the evil, and all the giants, for He is the King of Kings and Lord of Lords.

But the beast from the abyss comes forth with all its great horror and is given power to conquer. It is interesting that it says that he has *authority* over the nations but he can only *conquer* the saints. He has no authority over us. The only authority under which we live is the authority of Jesus Christ. The nations, the rebellious, the lost, live under the authority of satan. With us, he can sometimes exercise power, and sometimes he can even kill us. But he never has the authority. He only has authority over all those who worship the beast and all those whose names are not written in the Lamb's Book of Life.

The Number of the Beast: 666

At the end of chapter 13 we are introduced to this great 2,000-year-old mystery that every generation has sought to resolve: the number of the beast. The number that is his name is simply the number that represents man. In some ways, that is all we need to know. It tells us we are not looking for some kind of Godzilla to arrive. The beast comes in human form: 666 is the number of a man.

Initially it was the evil emperor Nero whose name and title in Hebrew characters totaled 666, for in ancient times all letters were assigned numerical values. Also, it is 666 because man and beast were created on the sixth day. He is 666 because Nebuchadnezzar, who, withstood the God of Heaven and said, "My own power and authority has done this," was turned into a beast. He lived out in the fields with the cattle. He ate grass. His hair grew like feathers and his nails like talons. God turned him into a beast. For he had set up a golden idol before which all had to bow, and it was 60 cubits high and 6 cubits wide. It was a 66 edifice that men would fall before to acknowledge Nebuchadnezzar as the ruler of the world.

The number six, is eternally less than seven, the number of completeness, and throughout Scripture it illustrates man's arrogant display of opposition to God's Kingdom. Og, the giant king of Bashan exercised his cruel dictatorship over a kingdom that consisted of 60 cities, all of which fell to the advancing forces of the armies of God. David, as he was about to bring in the kingdom and establish his rule in the world, had to overcome giants. Goliath was six cubits tall. David dealt with Goliath in his youth, and he killed him by crushing his head and finishing him off with his own sword. David's men killed five other giants who sought to resist the kingdom, totaling six in all. Four of them were Goliath's brothers, one of whom had six fingers on each hand and six toes on each foot. The last was a huge Egyptian, seven and a half feet tall (see 1 Chron. 11:23; 20:4-8).

We should note here an interesting spiritual strategy: God declared that the crushing of his head would bring about the destruction of the serpent. This is exactly what David did in his victory over Goliath. With his slingshot he struck the giant on the forehead, then to demonstrate his utter victory, he took the Philistine's own sword and severed his head. This sword that had once defiantly threatened the life of God's chosen king had now become David's own weapon of overcoming and victory. Later, one of David's mighty men, Benaiah who, like his lord, was also a giant slayer, conquered his adversary, a huge Egyptian, by snatching his spear and turning it into his own weapon of destruction. In an earlier chapter we looked at Habakkuk's song of the triumphs of God. He declared, "*You crushed the leader of the land of wickedness, You stripped him from head to foot. With his own spear You pierced his head*" (Hab. 3:13-14). The enemy's weapon of defiance is, by the power of God, turned into the weapon of his defeat.

The ultimate weapon that satan devised was the cross. It was to be the end of all the purposes of God. It was a cruel, wicked, hateful means of death. Satan hounded the seed of the woman to the cross. With a dark glint in his evil eye, satan rubbed his wicked hands together and thought, "Now I am going to win; now He is going to die." And Jesus carried the cross, the weapon devised by the evil one, to Golgotha. Now Golgotha means "hill of the skull." He took the cross to Skull Hill because Golgotha, for all intents and purposes, looked like the top of a human head. It looked like a skull. And when he got to the top of the hill, they took the weapon that satan had devised, and they thrust it into the ground and crushed the head. It was at Golgotha that the enemy was utterly defeated, and satan's weapon of destruction was turned upon himself!

The dragon, the beast, and the false prophet are all there to do us harm. The dragon is a nasty piece of work. The Bible tells us he is enormous. He is blood red because he is baptized in the blood of all those he has slain. He stands ready to devour. He stands with mouth open. He stands with demonic dribble hanging off his chin. He slavers with anticipation at the thought of devouring everyone. But every time he postures at you, every time he roars and snarls at you, revealing his fangs or unsheathing his claws, just remind him of this: he got beaten by a lamb! "You are just a poser!" tell him. "You got beaten by a lamb!" For the Lamb has triumphed over the dragon, and the Lamb will rule forever and ever. A dragon to devour us, a beast to dominate us, and a false prophet to deceive us, but God is with us to do us good.

We are more than conquerors through Him who loved us. He always leads us in triumphal procession in Christ Jesus, and, even if we die, our cry will be "*Where, O death, is your victory? Where, O death, is your sting?*" (1 Cor. 15:55).

CHAPTER 5

The Heavenly Woman

We have already referred to the woman who was about to give birth, who appears in chapter 12 of Revelation. Let us now take a closer look at her:

> *A great and wondrous sign appeared in Heaven: a woman clothed with the sun, with the moon under her feet and a crown of twelve stars on her head. She was pregnant and cried out in pain as she was about to give birth. Then another sign appeared in Heaven: an enormous red dragon with seven heads and ten horns and seven crowns on his heads. His tail swept a third of the stars out of the sky and flung them to the earth. The dragon stood in front of the woman who was about to give birth, so that he might devour her child the moment*

> *it was born. She gave birth to a son, a male child, who will rule all the nations with an iron scepter. And her child was snatched up to God and to His throne* (Revelation 12:1-5).

This heavenly woman is referred to as a great and wondrous sign. She is a sign like many other signs in Revelation, because that is how God has chosen to communicate with us through this book. But she is a "*great and wondrous sign.*" That is, she is a sign of special significance. This heavenly woman portrays something to us of the eternal purposes of God. Who is she? There are many answers to that question, and all of them are right! But in this chapter I will try to piece some of them together.

The Redeemed Community

First of all, her clothing gives us a hint as to who she is. She is clothed with the sun. She has 12 stars on her head, and under her feet is the moon. When we look into the Word of God, we find that there are people who are described in that same kind of way. Do you remember when Joseph had a dream of his ultimate authority? He dreamed of his own rise to power, and in his dream his father, mother, and brothers bowed down to worship him. In his dream he saw the sun, the moon, and 11 stars bowing down to him, and he was the twelfth star. The sun, the moon, and 12 stars represent the Israel of God. This is the beginning of the covenant community. This is the first generation of a nation that God is going to call his own, and it is described as the sun, the moon, and 12 stars. So, we are seeing God's historic purpose. We are seeing the beginnings of God's desire to bring His Word, His covenant, and His revelation to the ends of the earth. But the idea goes on to become more focused.

When we consider that wonderful poem in Scripture known as the Song of Solomon, we find a glorious love epic. It is the recounting of a relationship between the great king and the Shulammite maiden. It is speaking of the wooing and the winning by a king whose heart is captured by the beauty of the one he desires. Others join the chorus to give expression and meaning to the poem. It is full of significance. Song of Songs is not just a love manual; it testifies of Christ and is a picture of our relationship with Jesus. It is a picture of the bride and her response to the heavenly bridegroom. The friends who form the chorus of this great love song describe the maiden:

> *Who is this that appears like the dawn, fair as the moon, bright as the sun, majestic as the stars in procession?* (Song of Solomon 6:10)

Chapter 19 will speak to us specifically of the bride, but here, as in other parts of Revelation, we have a kind of pre-introduction for this woman in the heavens is also the bride. She represents the redeemed community, and it is the redeemed community in intimate relationship with her Lord.

Miracle Children

God's plan and purpose have always been to have His people bring forth spiritual offspring. When God created Adam and Eve, His mandate to them was to be fruitful, to multiply, and to fill the earth. God's will and purpose was that the whole earth would be populated with people just like Jesus.

That is God's eternal purpose. It has not changed. Just because down through the years people have failed, it does not mean for a minute that God has failed or adjusted his purpose or changed His plan. God is still seeking to fill the earth with his offspring.

In fact, God made it clear to Abraham that through His seed all the earth would be blessed (see Gen. 12:1-3). Have you noticed how God, in the Old Testament, introduces Himself as the God of Abraham, Isaac, and Jacob? That is how God makes Himself known. But there is an interesting thing about Abraham, Isaac, and Jacob. God confirmed His covenant with each one of them and promised each of them that through their seed His blessing would come to the earth. The most amazing thing about that is that Abraham, Isaac, and Jacob all married barren women. You would think that if God's purpose was to fill the earth with heavenly offspring, He would make sure that his servants married very fertile girls! But all of them married barren women. How strange, then, that God, who is looking for birth, increase, and multiplication, should choose to have His servants marry women who had no ability to reproduce. He's not exactly making it easy for himself! But the lesson it teaches us is important. The children that God wants to produce in the earth are all the result of miracles. God is looking for miracle children. God wants those who are born not in the natural way, but in a spiritual way.

When Jesus came into the world, John tells us,

> *He was in the world, and though the world was made through Him, the world did not recognize Him. He came to that which was His own, but His own did not receive*

> *Him. Yet to all who received Him, to those who believed in His name, He gave the right to become children of God—children born not of natural descent, nor of human decision or a husband's will, but born of God* (John 1:10-13).

The children that Jesus came to bring to life are miracle children. They are not just those who are born, they are those who are born again, born of the Spirit. God has always been seeking for Himself miracle children. When Israel had settled into the land, it was a very seesaw kind of history. Sometimes they were on the offensive and making great progress, and sometimes they were on the defensive and overpowered by the might of an enemy. God in His mercy and grace would raise up judges for them who would deliver them from the power of the enemy. One of the most remarkable judges raised up by God is a man called Samson. Samson, of course, was born of a woman who was barren. It was a miracle birth, because it is those who are born by miracle who are able to deliver God's people and fulfill God's purpose. God is looking for miracle children who will overcome the powers of darkness and who will bring in the Kingdom of God. One of the great works that Samson did was to pull down the temple of the foreign god and to see it collapse in absolute disarray, bringing death to his enemies and the land into a period of peace.

At another time when there was not much prophecy, when visions were rare, God answered the prayer of a barren woman and allowed her to conceive and bring forth a son. This boy would be dedicated to the Lord from his birth and would be brought up in the presence of God, in the environs of the tabernacle. His home was to be the place where God was, even though there was no word, and vision was rare. There was, nevertheless, a sense of God's presence. Before the lamp went out, God spoke to Samuel, raising him up and letting not one of His words fall to the ground. He established him as a prophet in the land, and he turned the people away from Philistine domination. This man was the forerunner of the Kingdom and the anointer of David, the man after God's own heart.

Hundreds of years later, darkness had again descended upon the nation; they were no longer under Philistine domination, but now the great power of Rome had devoured the people of God. There was no prophetic word. The last word that had been spoken by a prophet is recorded for us, and it is a sad and startling thing. If you go to the last book of the Old Testament and turn to the last chapter of the last book of the Old Testament and find the last verse in the last chapter of the last book, and read the last word in the last verse in the last chapter of the last book of the Old Testament, it is the word *curse* (see Mal. 4:6). What a terrible way to finish! What a terrible way to end! It is interesting then that when Jesus began his public ministry, the first word out of his mouth was *blessed.*

But the last prophetic word that came ringing from the heavens and reverberated in the ears of those who had ears to hear was "curse." Many years later, God answered the prayer of an old priest, and God had compassion on a woman who had been so long without children that her nickname was Barren (see Luke 1:36). She conceived and brought forth a son, John the Baptist, who would go before the Lord in the spirit and power of Elijah. The interesting thing about all three of those miracle boys is that each one of them was a Nazirite. Each one of them was dedicated solely to the Lord.

Samson, we are told, would be a Nazirite from his birth. It was said of Samuel that no razor would touch his head. That is one of the signs of the Nazirite. John, we are told, would drink no strong drink or alcohol. That is another sign of a Nazirite. These three men, dedicated to the Lord, committed to the Lord and His purpose, were miracle babies who brought in the Kingdom. For just as Samuel had anointed David as king, so John baptized Jesus and saw the Spirit of God coming upon him. They were forerunners of the Kingdom.

God has always been looking for the birth of miracle children who would bring in the Kingdom. Of course, the ultimate miracle child is not the one who is born out of a womb that is barren, but one that is born out of the womb of a virgin. So when we see this heavenly woman, we are seeing Manoah's wife, we are seeing Elizabeth, we are seeing Hannah, we are seeing those who bring forth the deliverer. And so we are, of course, seeing Mary. But in a sense we are also seeing more than that; we are seeing God's purpose acted out in a heavenly drama.

The Seed and the Serpent

When the curse came on the ground because of sin, there were also punishments inflicted on the man and on the woman who had sinned. The man would, by the toil and sweat of his brow, bring forth his bread. But *"to the woman He said, 'I will greatly increase your pains in childbearing; with pain you will give birth to children. Your desire will be for your husband, and he will rule over you'"* (Gen. 3:16).

This heavenly woman we see in Revelation 12 is in travail. She is in pain and is crying out. Her pain is greatly increased in her desire to bring forth children (see Gen. 3:16). So she is also Eve, the mother of all. But she is Eve in this sense: she is giving birth to the seed of the woman who will crush the serpent's head. This woman is in travail to bring forth the seed that will bring deliverance to a fallen world.

There are two kinds of children in our world, children of God and children of the devil. I am making that kind of statement continually because we need to understand that there is a clear and undeniable division between those who are of God and those who are not of God. There is no middle ground. There is no fuzzy edge. It is a clear-cut distinction between those who belong to God and those who do not. Jesus makes it very clear that even those who boasted in their ancestry, who said that they had Abraham as their father, were actually of their father the devil (see John 8:31-44). We can have no compromise. There has to be a clear distinction. That is one of the things that the Book of Revelation is about. Many still live in Babylon, but the call goes up, "*Come out of her, My people*" (Rev. 18:4). There is a sense of separation between that which is of God and that which is not of God. We have to maintain that separation, not in an exclusive and ghetto-type mentality that takes us away from the world; we are to be in the world, but not of the world; we are to be those who reach out to the world but do not compromise with the world.

In other words, we are to be like Jesus was. Jesus was accepted by sinners, but He was not affected by sinners. Jesus was not tainted by their sin, although He felt himself free and at liberty to go among them, because how can you win them if you are not among them? He maintained a clear distinction. The Bible tells us He was a friend of sinners, but it also says He was separate from sinners. That is how the Church has got to learn to be. We do not bring down our standards to make our message more acceptable to a sinful world. When the Spirit of God moved in the early church, when death came to Ananias and Sapphira, nobody dared join, but then it says the Lord added (see Acts 5:13-14)! We do not need to be afraid that our standards, our message, and our practices will be offensive to people. If we are doing it right, they will be! But if we are doing it right, God will add to us those who are being saved.

A Heavenly People

Returning to the woman in Revelation, we must note that she is located in the heavens. She is a heavenly woman. She is not earthbound, taken up with the affairs of this world. She is a woman who has her heart and her mind set on things that are above. The Church is a heavenly people. But it is more than this, even. The heavens speak not only of our destination but our origin. Let me explain.

The Book of Revelation is a book of contrasts. It is about two women, two cities. We find similar contrasts if we turn to the fourth chapter of Galatians. Paul is contending with a church that has become legalistic. There are two things that God despises: sin and legalism. When I read the Scriptures, it seems to me that He seems to despise legalism even more than sin. He hates legalism, and so Paul confronts the Galatians with their legalism and brings them a message from the Word. He brings them a picture from Scripture:

> *Tell me, you who want to be under the law, are you not aware of what the law says? For it is written that Abraham had two sons, one by the slave woman and the other*

> *by the free woman. His son by the slave woman was born in the ordinary way; but his son by the free woman was born as the result of a promise. These things may be taken figuratively, for the women represent two covenants. One covenant is from Mount Sinai and bears children who are to be slaves: This is Hagar. Now Hagar stands for Mount Sinai in Arabia and corresponds to the present city of Jerusalem, because she is in slavery with her children* (Galatians 4:21-25).

We must recognize that this is still true of the present city of Jerusalem: all who are born in it are born into slavery, not sonship.

> *But the Jerusalem that is above is free, and she is our mother. For it is written:*
>
> > *"Be glad, O barren woman, who bears no children; break forth and cry aloud, you who have no labor pains; because more are the children of the desolate woman than of her who has a husband."*
>
> *Now you, brothers, like Isaac, are children of promise. At that time the son born in the ordinary way persecuted the son born by the power of the Spirit. It is the same now. But what does the Scripture say? "Get rid of the slave woman and her son, for the slave woman's son will never share in the inheritance with the free woman's son." Therefore, brothers, we are not children of the slave woman, but of the free woman* (Galatians 4:26-31).

That Scripture refutes any idea that there is another way into the presence of God other than by miracle birth. The slave woman's son will never share in the inheritance. People from ethnic Israel will never share in the church's inheritance. That does not mean that there is no hope for Israel, for "*the grace of God that brings salvation has appeared to all men*" (Titus 2:11), and Paul's "*heart's desire and prayer to God for the Israelites* [was] *that they may be saved*" (Rom. 10:1). As the Kingdom increases in dimension and power, we must expect increasing numbers of Jews to be born again.

Who is this woman in the heavens, then? She is the Jerusalem that is from above, of which Paul speaks here; she is our mother. You and I have been born as part of the fulfillment of a promise. It is the promise that God made to Abraham, that through his seed all the earth would be blessed. But there is a greater promise even than that. It is a promise that God made to His Son. When Jesus went back into the presence of God and sat down at His right hand, the Father turned to Him and said, "*Ask of Me, and I will make the nations Your inheritance, the ends of the earth Your possession*" (Ps. 2:8).

God promised the world to Jesus, and you and I are the first fruits. You and I are the first demonstration that what God promised to Jesus is being fulfilled. We have come to birth. We have been born from above. When Jesus says to Nicodemus, "*You must be born again,*" that can legitimately be interpreted, "*You must be born from above.*" You and I were born from above. You and I have our origins in Heaven. I do not mean we were preexistent souls before our bodies came into being, but rather that our names were written in the Lamb's Book of Life before the world was created. You and I were born in Zion. God said He is going to write a list of those who were born in Zion (see Ps. 87:6), and you and I were born there. This heavenly woman is the Jerusalem that is from above.

When you realize who your mother is, you understand who you are. Israel was under pressure and in defeat. She was overcome by her enemies until Deborah arose as a mother in Israel. And as she arose, so her children found their strength, recovered their vitality, discovered their faith, moved on in power, and routed the enemy. It's good to know who your mother is.

The Covenant and the Offspring

We have been born from above, and this is not some kind of new departure. This has always been the purpose of God, right from the beginning, right from the Garden of Eden. God wanted the world filled with his offspring. Earlier I mentioned the last word that Malachi spoke, but, praise God, he said other things, some of them blessing and some of them rebuke. One of the things that he rebuked his generation for was their forsaking of the covenant. When Paul used the picture of Sarah and Hagar, he said that they are two covenants. So, the women represent covenants. They also represent mountains, and they represent the sons they brought forth. There is this kind of contrast all the way through the Scriptures: of cities, sons, women, and mountains. But one of the confrontations that Malachi brings to his generation is that they have forsaken the covenant. He tells them that they forsook the covenant with Levi. The covenant with Levi is the covenant with Moses, who was of the tribe of Levi, and it had to do with religious observance and legal requirements. Malachi admonishes them:

> *"And you will know that I have sent you this admonition so that My covenant with Levi may continue," says the*

> *Lord Almighty. "My covenant was with him, a covenant of life and peace, and I gave them to him; this called for reverence and he revered Me and stood in awe of My name. True instruction was in his mouth and nothing false was found on his lips. He walked with Me in peace and uprightness, and turned many from sin. "For the lips of a priest ought to preserve knowledge, and from his mouth men should seek instruction—because he is the messenger of the Lord Almighty. But you have turned from the way* (Malachi 2:4-8).

He said, "I made a covenant with you. It was a covenant of life and a covenant of peace, but you turned from the way. You have broken the covenant." And when you break the covenant with God, everything begins to crumble. The domino effect sets in, and trouble arises. So he confronts them, not only with their breaking of covenant with God, but with their breaking of covenant with one another:

> *Have we not all one Father? Did not one God create us? Why do we profane the covenant of our fathers by breaking faith with one another?* (Malachi 2:10)

Once you have broken covenant with God, it is an easy step to break covenant with your brother. So society has come under pressure. When our relationship with God breaks down, society begins to unravel. We see it in our own nation and in the world. Although there was not an awareness of covenant, there was once an awareness of godliness, of responsibility, an awareness that there was one who sat as judge. There was, at least, an acknowledgment of a God over the earth, but when that was eroded, society began to collapse. This breakdown was inevitable because God has made covenant the building block of our society. Society begins with our relationship with Him. When that has broken down, our relationship with one another breaks down.

Malachi continues:

> *Another thing you do: You flood the Lord's altar with tears. You weep and wail because He no longer pays attention to your offerings or accepts them with pleasure from your hands. You ask, "Why?" It is because the Lord is acting as the witness between you and the wife of your youth, because you have broken faith with her, though she is your partner, the wife of your marriage covenant* (Malachi 2:13-14).

When we break covenant with God, and with one another, it is easy for marriage to start to collapse. You can trace that in the social history of our own nation and many others. So God says, "I am the God of covenant, and I want to bring you into covenant. I want you to be in covenant with me. I want you to be in covenant with one another. I want you to be in covenant with the wife of your youth." And why is God looking for that and demanding it? What motivates him to place so much importance on it? The answer is in the very next verse:

> *Has not the Lord made them one? In flesh and spirit they are His. And why one? Because He was seeking godly offspring* (Malachi 2:15).

God has always been looking for godly offspring. He has been looking for his bride to bring forth his sons. The tragedy of Israel, of old covenant Israel, is that because they broke covenant, they were unable to do that. They failed to do what God wanted them to do. Consider how Isaiah describes it:

> *As a woman with child and about to give birth writhes and cries out in her pain, so were we in Your presence, O Lord. We were with child, we writhed in pain, but we gave birth to wind. We have not brought salvation to the earth; we have not given birth to people of the world* (Isaiah 26:17-18).

What a tragic confession! What a dreadful anticlimax, to go through all the agonies of a phantom pregnancy, to go through the travail of one who is going to give birth and to produce nothing but wind! That is the history of Israel. God was looking for godly offspring, but no children were born. God was looking not only for a multitude of godly offspring, but for a specific offspring. The Bible takes two great Old Testament expectations and changes them radically in the hands of Paul. He promised Abraham two things: land and children. But, in Romans, Paul tells us that God actually promised Abraham and his offspring that they would be heirs to the world, not to a small piece of land in the Middle East (see Rom. 4:13). Then, in Galatians, Paul is talking about Abraham's seed and remarks, "*The promises were spoken to Abraham and to his seed. The Scripture does not say 'and to seeds,' meaning many people, but 'and to your seed,' meaning one person, who is Christ*" (Gal. 3:16).

So Paul takes the promise which had geographical limitation, takes the limitations off it, and says, "God wants to give you the world." Then he takes the broad and general interpretation about seed or offspring and specifies it and restricts it to one. That one is Christ. The promises of Abraham, then, are not for Palestine but for the world. We do not have to get into the debate over whose land it is, whether it belongs to the

Palestinians or to the Jews. It belongs to God, and, ultimately, because it belongs to God, it belongs to us. And the seed is not many but one, Christ.

A Savior Is Born

The promise about the offspring, then, is not fulfilled in ethnic Israel. It is fulfilled in Jesus, and we see from this dramatic picture in the Book of Revelation that it is Jesus who is being brought forth, for He is snatched up to the throne, where He rules the nations with an iron rod. He is the ultimate overcomer, and He will bring God's Kingdom to the nations. This was the expectation in the prophets. Although they knew Israel had failed, many of them believed that God would do what He said He would do, that God's plan would ultimately be fulfilled, and that His purpose would prosper. And so we hear from the prophet Micah,

> *But you, Bethlehem Ephrathah, though you are small among the clans of Judah, out of you will come for Me one who will be ruler over Israel, whose origins are from of old, from ancient times. Therefore Israel will be abandoned until the time when she who is in labor gives birth and the rest of His brothers return to join the Israelites. He will stand and shepherd His flock in the strength of the Lord, in the majesty of the name of the Lord His God. And they will live securely, for then His greatness will reach to the ends of the earth. And He will be their peace. When the Assyrian invades our land and marches through our fortresses, we will raise against him seven shepherds, even eight leaders of men* (Micah 5:2-5).

There is a birth coming. They knew it. They expected it. When the men from the East came inquiring where the Christ was to be born, Herod's advisers used this Scripture to prove that the Christ would be born in Bethlehem. Here was this great expectation: that she who was in travail would bring forth a son. You see, God's will and purpose was always for sons, but most specifically it was for His Son to be born into the world. And what we are seeing here is a reenactment of all those women who gave birth to deliverers down through the ages until ultimately Jesus Himself comes, the magnificent Deliverer, the mighty Savior. He has now come to bring deliverance. The serpent is there. The dragon is there, waiting to devour Him, just as he stood to devour Moses. Here he is seeking to snatch the child, but God snatches Him instead! This picture tells us nothing of Jesus' ministry, of His miracles, or of His death. He goes from birth to resurrection in an instant, in order that it might be understood that God's ultimate purpose is for Him to rule all the nations.

Isaiah had said to a king under pressure and in despair because of invading armies, "*Ask the Lord your God for a sign, whether in the deepest depths or in the highest heights*" (Isa. 7:11). The king did not ask, but God gave it anyway. In this twelfth chapter of Revelation we see this sign: a sign in the heavens. And the sign was of a woman giving birth: "*Therefore the Lord himself will give you a sign: The virgin will be with child and will give birth to a son, and will call Him Immanuel*" (Isa. 7:14).

You see, although Jesus is eternal, Jesus has an earthly history. We do, too. We have a heavenly history because our names were written in the Lamb's Book of Life before the world was ever made. But we also have an earthly history. We are in the church because God wrote our names and He chose us in Christ before the foundation of the world (see Eph. 1:4; Rev. 13:8). But there was also a moment in history when we heard and responded to the Gospel. Jesus is the same. He has a heavenly history because He is the eternal God. But He has an earthly history because there was a time when He was born into the world. What we are seeing is the heavenly and earthly coming together in the purposes of God.

This tells us that the whole point of His birth was that He would rule the nations with an iron scepter. That is a fulfillment of many Old Testament Scriptures. First of all, Genesis tells us that "*The scepter will not depart from Judah, nor the ruler's staff from between his feet, until he comes to whom it belongs and the obedience of the nations is his*" (Gen. 49:10). The psalmist tells us that God says, "*I will make the nations Your inheritance, the ends of the earth Your possession. You will rule them with an iron scepter*" (Ps. 2:8-9). But the interesting thing is that that is the exact promise that Jesus made to the church at Thyatira. We also, who are born from above, are caught up to the throne, as He promised the Laodiceans, and rule the nations with an iron scepter, as He promised the Thyatirans. We also are born and ascend and sit on the throne.

We are included in another sense, too. We are not only the child that is born but the mother that brings forth the child. It is a bit confusing, but it does also say of Jesus that He was both the Root and the Offspring of David. He is the Root of David because David was chosen in God's eternal will; but Jesus, in terms of human history, came from the line of David. Our job, in a sense, is to bring Christ to the world; Christ, so to speak, is to be birthed through us, the Church, so that the world might see Him. This is what Jesus said to His disciples:

> *I tell you the truth, you will weep and mourn while the world rejoices. You will grieve, but your grief will turn to joy. A woman giving birth to a child has pain because her time has come; but when her baby is born she forgets the anguish because of her joy that a child is born into the world. So with you: Now is your time of grief, but I will see you again and you will rejoice, and no one will take away your joy* (John 16:20-22).

Jesus is saying, "I am going to die, but you are going to suffer. And the suffering and pain that you experience is just like a woman giving birth because as you identify with me in my suffering, you are bringing forth the purposes of God." You and I are here to give birth to sons in this the world. Paul puts it in these terms to the Galatians:

> *My dear children, for whom I am again in the pains of childbirth until Christ is formed in you* (Galatians 4:19).

Have you given birth lately? Have you felt the birth pangs? God wants to use you to bring forth redemptive and ruling sons, sons who will share the throne and have authority over the nations. It is time for Zion to bring forth her sons to the glory of God.

CHAPTER 6

The Exodus Paradigm

We cannot fully understand the implications of the New Testament if we do not have a grounding in the Old Testament because the Old Testament is the basis for New Testament revelation. That is why it is very important that we become familiar with the Old Testament Scriptures: Not only did God base New Testament revelation on the Old Testament, He based later writings in the Old Testament on earlier writings. When you read the prophets, they speak of future events in terms of past activities and certain things that God did in the early days of man's history that became part of the prophetic vision. For example, the idea of "the garden," from that first Garden of Eden, becomes a repetitive theme in Scripture and a picture of what God will do for his people. "The flood" becomes a repetitive picture of God's judgment. "The Egyptian captivity," in particular, becomes a paradigm of God's salvation purposes. This is true all the way through the Word of God. It is true in the prophets, in the whole New Testament, and particularly in the Book of Revelation. Revelation is jam-packed full of Old Testament stories, references, and allusions. It is full of all that God has done in the past, but it brings it right up to date, declaring that what God has done, He is still doing and He will yet do.

I have mentioned more than once that this book really is a book about the first century. In fact, many times it talks about things that "must soon take place" or are "about to take place" (see Rev. 1:1,19; 22:6; see also 2:16; 3:11; 11:4; 22:7,12,20), and when John wrote that down, under the dictation of Jesus, he was not thinking that "soon" meant in 2,000 years time. There was an immediacy to these prophecies that was understood by the first-generation believers who could see it being fulfilled in their day as God shook off unrepentant and covenant-breaking Israel. But as we have said, what God has done is a picture of what God is doing and is going to do. What John is writing about is both a fulfillment of prophecy and a prophetic declaration of things yet to happen.

There are many hints, visions, and glimpses in the Book of Revelation of the Exodus era—perhaps more than of any other period in Old Testament history. The Exodus becomes, to the prophets, a picture of God's redemptive purposes. That helps us to understand the very crux of the Book of Revelation. It is not just a book of punishment, of judgment, of God's wrath being poured out onto a wayward world. It is a redemptive book. It is a book about a God who saves, delivers, and redeems his people. So in this chapter we will consider several episodes where Exodus is revisited in the Book of Revelation.

Sacrifice

The first thing that we need to realize is the similarity between Exodus and Revelation, in terms of the sacrifice God made. When he is bringing greetings from Jesus and the Father and the seven spirits, John tells us about Jesus that He has "*freed us from our sins by His blood*" (Rev. 1:5). This is a very deliberate choice of words. The implication is that sin was bondage, imprisonment, slavery, and that we are freed by Jesus' blood. This is a great and wonderful truth. God did not just forgive your sin. He freed you from it! Some versions say that He "separated us from our sin." That is what God has done, and if believers could understand the implications of that, many of them would not live the powerless lives that they are leading. In the Old Testament, all the blood of sacrifice could do was to cover and forgive your sin; it could not deal with the power of sin. It dealt with the penalty, but it had no influence over the power. Men could find sacrifice that took away their sins, but not sacrifice that could keep them from sinning. So a man would go into the temple, make his sacrifice, be pronounced forgiven, and go back into a hostile environment that almost immediately led him to sin again.

When Abraham took Isaac up the mountain to sacrifice him, Isaac was an astute young man. He was not a boy; he was probably in his late teens or early twenties. He could have fought against the man who was over 100 years old and overcome him, but he himself was very submissive. He had the same faith that his father had. He believed in resurrection. At least he did when he got there, but to begin with, he was not sure what was going on. He had the wood on the shoulder as he ascended the hill, and we can imagine him saying to his dad, "Father, we have got the wood and the knife and the fire, but where is the lamb?" And that question has echoed all the way down through history: "Where is the lamb? Where is the lamb that can deliver us from sin?" Abraham's response was that God would provide a lamb. There was a longing and an expectation from that moment on for a lamb that God would provide.

As you know, when God came down to deliver His people, to set them free from Egyptian bondage, He did it by the blood of a lamb. Each household was to have its sacrificial lamb. That is why we can say with confidence that when we preach the Gospel, we declare good news "to you and your house": our expectation should be whole household conversions. We believe that salvation took place household by household, a lamb for each house. They had to take the lamb, by the way, into their home so that sacrificing it would be a painful operation: Here was a lamb that had lived as one of the family! Here was a lamb that had lived like a cuddly pet in the house, and now its throat was to be cut, its blood to be shed and put on the lintels and the doorposts. But it was the blood of a lamb that would set them free, that would separate them from the powers of darkness and the cruelty of the Egyptian taskmasters. It was the lamb that would open the door out of slavery and bring them into the glorious liberty of the sons of God. This was a lamb that would free them from their slavery and their oppression. They came out by the blood of a lamb. God said, "*When I see the blood, I will pass over you*" (Exod. 12:13).

When the tabernacle and temple system of sacrifice was initiated, there were many sacrifices, but the Israelites knew even then that the blood of bulls or goats could not take away sin (see Ps. 40:6; 51:16-17). They were still crying in their hearts, "Where is the lamb?" and the prophet Isaiah, under the anointing of God, spoke of a lamb, dumb before his shearers. He spoke of a lamb that bore our sicknesses and carried our infirmities, by whose stripes we would be healed (see Isa. 53:4-7). He spoke about Jesus. Many years later, in the middle of a desert, a eunuch read this prophecy about the suffering lamb. He asked Philip, "Is he talking about himself or somebody else?" Then, beginning at that very Scripture, Philip told him about Jesus. Every sacrifice in the Old Testament had pointed to Jesus. Every sacrificial lamb was a forerunner of the Lamb of God.

Jesus describes John the Baptist as someone who is more than a prophet (see Matt. 11:9). That is a very elevated place to occupy, for the prophets were great men, anointed servants of God. But Jesus said that John was more than a prophet. Why? When you read about John, you discover two interesting things. Firstly, he only had one sermon. All he ever said was, "Repent, for the Kingdom of Heaven is at hand." And secondly, the Scripture tells us clearly and distinctly that John did no miracles. He had no miracles and one sermon! And yet Jesus said that he was the most important of them all. He was most important for this reason: it falls to John, in that long line of prophetic ministries that prophesied of things to come, to stand by the roadside, see Jesus coming, point to Him, and say: "*Look, the Lamb of God, who takes away the sin of the world!*" (John 1:29). All the way down through history they had been crying, "Where is the lamb?" and John comes and declares, "Here is the Lamb!" The greatest ministry that we can fulfill is simply to point people to the Lamb. The Book of Revelation points us to the Lamb: the elders tell John that "*the Lion of the tribe of Judah…has triumphed,*" and John turns and looks and declares "*I saw a Lamb, looking as if it had been slain*" (Rev. 5:5-6). He is standing there as our Passover sacrifice because it is his blood that frees us from our sin and as the Apostle Paul writes to the Corinthians: "*Christ, our Passover lamb, has been sacrificed*" (1 Cor. 5:7).

The favorite title that John uses for Jesus throughout the Book of Revelation is "the Lamb." What the Book of Revelation does is to take us back to the great deliverance that God wrought for us by the sacrifice that He made through the blood of the Lamb. Not only did His blood free us from our sin, it purchased us for God. So you and I now belong exclusively to God. We are not our own. We are bought with a price.

Salvation Secured

Not only did Jesus make sacrifice for us, but He secured salvation for us. It is not necessarily the same thing. Do you know you can be born again and not saved? You can come to Jesus, repent, and believe on Him, but then be a slave of fear. You can be a Christian, have your name written in the Book of Life, but then be a slave to unbreakable habits. You can be born again but not saved from things that defile, that imprison, and that bind you. I am not talking about being ensnared by demons or inhabited by fallen powers, but I am talking about being under the influence of things outside of yourself that cause you to be a prisoner. Christ frees you. The great ministry of Jesus was to declare liberty to the captives.

It is an interesting thing that, although Israel was rescued from Egypt by the blood of the lamb, Pharaoh pursued them. He had animosity in his heart towards the people of God. Scripture speaks of Pharaoh as a shadowy type of the dragon, and of the beast out of the sea, so he could not help but feel animosity in his heart against the woman and the seed of the woman. He had to follow his nature and inclination. He could not let the people go. He had to pursue them and seek to destroy them. We have seen in the twelfth chapter of Revelation that the dragon is seeking to destroy the woman and her child, but the child is caught up into the heavens and satan is cast down out of the heavens. Then it tells us:

> *When the dragon saw that he had been hurled to the earth, he pursued the woman who had given birth to the male child. The woman was given the two wings of a great eagle, so that she might fly to the place prepared for her in the desert, where she would be taken care of for a time, times and half a time, out of the serpent's reach* (Revelation 12:13-14).

The devil pursues the seed of the woman, but God rescues her. In one commentary I have read on this particular passage, the author maintains that the wings of a great eagle obviously represent the United States Air Force, and there is coming a time when the godly power of America will rescue Jews from their persecution and airlift them into the desert regions of America and Canada that are as yet unoccupied but have been reserved for a Jewish people to find relief from physical opposition. And he was serious! This is stuff that is put forward as a serious interpretation of this Scripture. But is it true? Is the eagle with wings a picture of the United States Air Force? Or is there something else in Scripture that would help us understand what is going on here? Let us go back to the Exodus incident and see what God says about His people:

> *You yourselves have seen what I did to Egypt, and how I carried you on eagles' wings and brought you to myself* (Exodus 19:4).

God rescued Israel on eagles' wings. And the prophet Isaiah tells us that he will do the same for us:

> *But those who hope in the Lord will renew their strength. They will soar on wings like eagles; they will run and not grow weary, they will walk and not be faint* (Isaiah 40:31).

God moves to lift us up out of our despair, our captivity and our oppression under the power of the evil one. God is committed to our utter salvation and our total liberty. He has committed Himself to that. He lifts us up on eagles' wings.

This is a wonderful picture that we find again in Deuteronomy, where it is especially interesting:

> *In a desert land He found him, in a barren and howling waste. He shielded him and cared for him; He guarded him as the apple of His eye, like an eagle that stirs up its nest and hovers over its young, that spreads its wings to catch them and carries them on its pinions. The Lord alone led him; no foreign god was with him* (Deuteronomy 32:10-12).

The interesting thing about this particular Scripture is that some of the words are almost exactly the words that Moses uses to describe the creation, when the Spirit of God hovered over the deep. Just as the initial creation is described as barren and empty, so too is the wilderness where God found his people and hovered over them. Just as the great eagle Spirit of God hovered over the deep and, out of the darkness and void, brought forth creation in all its glory, so God now hovers over a people to cause them to become a new creation. Jesus used a similar image when He stood up, looked at the city, and said, "*O Jerusalem, Jerusalem, you who kill the prophets and stone those sent to you, how often I have longed to gather your children together, as a hen gathers her chicks under her wings, but you were not willing*" (Matt. 23:37).

God secures us from all the power of the enemy, from the visitations of judgment, and from all the power of Egypt, by lifting us out of it all on wings like eagles, by taking us to a place where we will be cared for, where we are not abandoned, not deserted in the desert, not left to wander in the wilderness, but taken care of, fed, watered, equipped, and strengthened. God cares for us, and God moves on our behalf to secure our salvation just as He led His people through the wilderness.

Safety Guaranteed

In the Book of Revelation, the dragon pursues the woman spewing out rivers of water in order to carry her away in the flood. But God keeps her safe. In fact, it tells us that the earth helps the woman (see Rev. 12:16). We need to understand that the earth is on our side. It is God's earth, and therefore it is His servant, and it does His will. Note that the earth opens its mouth and swallows the river that could have destroyed the woman.

Consider what happened when Israel was in the wilderness, when there arose among the people a rebellion led by Korah. Very often that which arises internally is far more deadly than that which attacks us from outside. The foe within is more to be feared than the foe without. Now Korah felt that he should be at least the equal of Moses, believing that God had made the whole congregation holy and that they were therefore all priests. He wanted to do what was reserved for the Aaronic priesthood. This was a rebellion and a challenge, and God made it very clear that He would not abide challenges to His authority, nor rebellion against those whom He has raised up in leadership. And so the earth opened up its mouth and swallowed what would have become a river of corruption that would have destroyed not only what God wanted to do in, for, and through His people, but also the ability of God's people to fulfill His purposes—all this before they ever got into the land.

Now we saw how the dragon is associated with the waters when we were considering the beast that came up out of the sea, and we saw how Rahab, the great Egyptian king, was also identified with that beast. Here, then, we are seeing the dragon using the weapons of his warfare, spewing out waters that are geared to destroying God's people.

Although not speaking directly of the Exodus, but about the situation in his own time and generation, the prophet speaks in these terms and prophetically applies it in every generation: "*I am against you, Pharaoh king of Egypt, you great monster lying among your streams*" (Ezek. 29:3).

And this is the dragon, Pharaoh, sending forth his streams to destroy the church of Christ and being utterly frustrated. God has lifted us out of his reach and opened the earth so that his violence is dissipated and comes to no effect.

One of the things that is revisited in the Book of Revelation has to do with the sentences that He passed on that nation. The plagues that we find in the Book of Revelation are almost an action replay of the plagues that were experienced in Egypt. This is one of the ways that God communicates to us that history is prophetic. The judgments that He poured down on Egypt were not just on the Egyptians but on the gods of Egypt, to break their power and to release His people, and these are the very things that are reenacted in the Book of Revelation.

The first of the bowls of wrath is poured out on the land and produces ugly and painful sores, matching the fifth plague on Egypt, which was festering boils. The second bowl of wrath is poured out onto the sea, and the sea becomes blood; that was the first plague that Moses called down on Egypt, turning the waters of the Nile to blood. The third is like it, wrath on rivers and springs, and they, too, turn to blood. The fourth is wrath on the sun, bringing intense heat; we do not find any obvious equivalent to this one in the plagues poured on Egypt. The next, though, is wrath on the throne of the beast, bringing darkness and plague; this is the eighth plague of Exodus, where darkness comes on the whole nation except on the place where the people of God are living. The sixth bowl is wrath on the river Euphrates, and the river Euphrates dries up; this is a kind of reversal of the miracle of the Red Sea, for the Red Sea was dried up for God's people to pass over, but now the Euphrates is dried up for the enemies to come. As the Euphrates dries up, foul frog spirits come to deceive the whole world, just as in the second plague on Egypt frogs came up and covered the land. The seventh bowl is wrath poured out on the air resulting in lightning, thunder, earthquake, and a great hailstorm, which was the sixth plague that God sent down on the Egyptians.

It is easy to see the parallels. God's plagues are coming on nations that are disobedient. The other Exodus plagues, those of gnats and flies, are surely seen again in those locusts that we considered in an earlier chapter, who come flying out of the pit, an airborne pestilence, flying demons who come to terrify and overcome those who are the enemies of God. So we find these terrible Egyptian plagues and visitations being reenacted first of all on unrepentant, covenant-breaking Israel, but then upon all people who rebel against God in their hearts. We must remember, of course, that these are pictures, symbols, and signs, not literal visitations.

It is important to note that if you put the trumpets and the bowls next to each other, you will find that they are the same things seen from a different angle. For instance, the first trumpet and the first bowl have to do with the earth. The second trumpet and the second bowl have to do with the sea. The third trumpet and bowl have to do with rivers and springs. The fourth of each have to do with the lights in the heavens. The fifth have to do with either creatures coming out of the abyss or God darkening and afflicting the throne of the beast. The sixth in both have to do with the river Euphrates, and the seventh have to do with the earthquake, manifestations of God's power, and voices from Heaven. There is a repetition with increased intensity.

I should also point out that the sevens in Revelation are almost always divided into the first four and the remaining three. Let us look at the first four, because these have to do with humanity and the last three usually have to do with demon powers. When the angels pour out their judgments on the earth, it affects the comfort of men and women. It disrupts their lifestyle and spoils the place where they live. It interrupts their comfort and confidence. Hail, fire, and blood are poured out from the sky. When the sea is affected, it does not just affect the creatures that live in the sea, but rather the maritime enterprises of the world. It is a picture of commerce being affected. When the rivers and springs are being focused upon, it is sign that human satisfaction and contentment are being affected, for these are the things that give us life. The Bible says that all our springs of joy are in Zion. We read that there is a river whose springs make glad the city of God. But here are rivers and springs that are defiled, and the contentment that is experienced in life is suddenly gone. Then, when the sun, the moon, and the stars are darkened and men cannot see by their light, confidence has gone, and confusion has come because they can no longer see clearly or understand properly.

So when these things come on the earth, we are not looking for literal buckets of blood to come falling out of the sky (see Rev. 8:7). Rather, we are seeing the fulfillment of the statement of the Israelites at the time of Jesus' arrest, when they said, "*Let His blood be on us*" (Matt. 27:25; see also Ps. 7:16). It is now figuratively coming upon their heads, and their comfort is being removed. God interferes with the commerce of godless men as He destroys the trading fleets of the nations.

God deals with that sense of contentment and well-being in the human heart as rivers that once were sparkling streams of satisfaction are now turned to putrefying blood. God affects men's confidence and ability to see and to understand and to make right decisions as He brings darkness where once there was light. These are the things that God does and that the plagues speak to us of. It is to shake the confidence of those who are affected by them. It is to make them aware that things are not well and that if they had any sense at all, they would seek the Lord while He may be found and call upon Him while He is near.

Singers of Songs

The fourth thing that is very important for us to understand relates to the song that they sing. In the fifteenth chapter of Revelation, we see a sea of glass mixed with fire. Now if you were to see a sea of glass mixed with fire, it would look like a red sea. Beside the sea were those who had been victorious over the beast just as Israel came through the Red Sea and was free of the beast of Egypt. They sang a song, the song of Moses, the servant of God, and the song of the Lamb. Those who came through the Red Sea were led in song by Moses:

> *Then Moses and the Israelites sang this song to the Lord:*
>
> *"I will sing to the Lord, for He is highly exalted. The horse and its rider He has hurled into the sea"* (Exodus 15:1).

We sing the same song, the song of Moses and of the Lamb, because we have been through the Red Sea. We have all been baptized into Jesus in the sea and in the cloud. We have all been made to drink of the same spiritual drink (see 1 Cor. 10:1-4). We are God's redeemed and spirit-filled people.

It is the same for us with the sustenance they received. God promised this to Moses: "I will rain down bread from Heaven for you." God is the God who supplies all of our needs. He is the God who is committed to our well-being. He is committed to supply miraculously when natural abilities have failed. God fed His people through the wilderness, and Jesus says to one of the churches in Revelation, "*To him who overcomes, I will give some of the hidden manna*" (Rev. 2:17). We feast upon the same bread of Heaven. We eat angels' food in the pilgrimage upon which God has sent us forth. Just as Israel in the wilderness was fed again and again, so we are always fed the bread of Heaven. Jesus said, "*The bread of God is He who comes down from Heaven and gives life to the world....I am the bread of life. He who comes to Me will never go hungry*" (see John 6:25-35). We feast on Him in our hearts and are filled with His goodness.

In Exodus, God said, "*I will dwell among the Israelites and be their God*" (Exod. 29:45). That is part of the covenant statement. But here God is saying, "I will dwell among them." He pitched His tent right where they were. Israel lived in tents. That is why they celebrated the Feast of Booths. They lived in tents in all their journeying through the wilderness, and so did God. God camped with them. The Book of Revelation declares, "*The dwelling of God is with men, and He will live with them. They will be His people, and God himself will be with them and be their God*" (Rev. 21:3). That was prefigured with God in the presence of His people in the wilderness, and now he is with us in power, for "*They are before the throne of God and serve*

Him day and night in His temple; and He who sits on the throne will spread His tent over them. Never again will they hunger; never again will they thirst" (Rev. 7:15-16).

There are people who serve Him day and night. The Scripture says, "*You will be for Me a kingdom of priests*" (Exod. 19:6). Well, we have already seen that that is the very status that we occupy. We are God's Exodus people. We are God's true Israel. We are those among whom He dwells and who are called to serve Him. What God has done, God will yet do, and if you feel yourself imprisoned, captured, chained, or restricted, then there is a God who will set you free. There is blood that has been shed that frees you from sin. If you are under pressure, then there are wings that will lift you, for God is with us and God is our Savior. If you are hungry, there is bread from Heaven, hidden manna, that will sustain you, water from the rock that will refresh you, for that which was "natural" has in Christ become a spiritual reality.

CHAPTER 7

In the Winepress

In this chapter, I would like us to consider two passages from the Book of Revelation. You will need to read 14:14-20 and 19:11-16. I want to suggest that these two passages concern the same act seen from two different angles. In one, we have the Lord seated on a white cloud. In the other, He is seated on His heavenly white stallion. Both of them are white with the purity of God's purpose. In the one, He wears a crown on His head because He is the King of Heaven. In the other, as he rides forth on his horse, he has many crowns because He is king of all the kings of the earth. He takes the crowns of the nations as He rides victoriously through His world and puts them upon His own head. As the reaper He has a sickle, and as the warrior He has a sword, but each represents the same idea and concept. In one He is going out to subdue the nations, and in the other He is reaping the harvest of the world. The same themes and concepts, though, are presented to us in both, and in both we see the winepress of God's wrath and the trampling of the grape harvest of our world.

The Vineyard

This grape or vine image is of incredible importance in Scripture. In the earlier chapter about the heavenly woman we saw that the Shulammite maiden, the loved one of the Book of Song of Solomon, was related to the sun, the moon, and the stars. If you read it carefully, you will discover that the whole Book of Song of Songs is about a vineyard. In fact, it begins by her saying, "*My own vineyard I have neglected*" (Song of Sol. 1:6): she initially was negligent. But then it ends with her saying that she will bring the produce of her fruitful vineyard to the king. The book progresses from a vineyard that is neglected to a vineyard that is fruitful and profitable. This picture of the vineyard is one repeated right through Scripture, and it is one by which God communicates important truths to us.

When Noah came out of the ark into a new earth and under a new Heaven, the first thing he did was to plant a vineyard (see Gen. 9:20). In fact, not only was it the first thing he did, Scripture actually tells us he was the first to ever plant a vineyard. He was the creator, if you like, of the vineyard culture. And it is interesting that it was the first thing God wanted him to do when he resettled the planet, when he was to reinhabit the earth. The vineyard was to be the symbol of this new earth, of a new people who would fill this earth.

When God brought His people into Canaan, He spoke of them as those planted in the land like a vineyard (see Isa. 5:1-7). God's people were His vineyard. Interestingly, when God first wanted them to go in and take the land, when they were at Kadesh Barnea, He had them send out spies to see what the land was like. God's desire for them was that they would respond in faith and go in and take the land, but there were giants there, and it filled them with fear and trepidation. However, they did fulfill their task of spying out the land, and they came back with a single cluster of grapes so huge that took two of them to carry it. It was the time of the first ripe grapes, and it was God's intention that Israel would take the land at grape harvest. They were to move into the land when the grapes were ripe.

Now this helps us to understand the imagery of the winepress, because for Israel it meant victory, while for Canaan it meant that they were going to be vanquished. Consistently throughout Scripture, we see that a single act can mean both life and death to different people. For one, it is coming into their inheritance; for the other it is being dispossessed. God planned for that to happen. His original intention was that at the time that the grapes were harvested and the wine was being produced in the winepress, His people would possess their promised land.

Let me take you to a Scripture in Isaiah that speaks of how God viewed His people in Canaan:

> *I will sing for the one I love a song about his vineyard: My loved one had a vineyard on a fertile hillside* (Isaiah 5:1).

It is significant that it is like a garden and it is on a hillside. The Garden of Eden was on a mountain. It certainly had to be on an elevated for rivers to flow out of it. So the garden where God displayed His glory was on a hill; and from there His life was to flow out to the ends of the earth. By the way, when Elijah had a confrontation with the prophets of Baal and called down the manifestation of the power of God on Mount Carmel, the name Carmel actually means orchard: the confrontation was actually in an orchard on a mountain.

Jesus told his disciples, "*My Father is the gardener. . . . I am the vine; you are the branches*" (John 15:1-5). God is concerned to reproduce His garden. It has always been His purpose. It is interesting to note that when Jesus died, He died in a garden; when Jesus was buried, He was buried in a garden (see John 19:41). This is not chance or coincidence. It is the plan and purpose of God. He wants us to know that He is concerned about the garden. When Jesus rose from the dead and Mary saw Him, she thought He was the gardener. Well, she was actually quite close—He is the gardener's Son! The Father is the great gardener. He plants gardens. We are called "*oaks of righteousness, a planting of the Lord*" (Isa. 61:3). God has got what we Brits call green fingers! He is always planting His people. Although He created the world with a word, when He wanted somewhere for Adam to live, He planted a garden. He got His hands down in the dirt, and He planted a garden. And then He planted the man in the garden. In Isaiah we see that He has His people planted on a fertile hillside.

> *He dug it up and cleared it of stones and planted it with the choicest vines. He built a watchtower in it and cut out a winepress as well. Then he looked for a crop of good*

> *grapes, but it yielded only bad fruit. "Now you dwellers in Jerusalem and men of Judah, judge between me and my vineyard. What more could have been done for my vineyard than I have done for it? When I looked for good grapes, why did it yield only bad? Now I will tell you what I am going to do to my vineyard: I will take away its hedge, and it will be destroyed; I will break down its wall, and it will be trampled. I will make it a wasteland, neither pruned nor cultivated, and briers and thorns will grow there. I will command the clouds not to rain on it." The vineyard of the Lord Almighty is the house of Israel, and the men of Judah are the garden of His delight. And He looked for justice, but saw bloodshed; for righteousness, but heard cries of distress* (Isaiah 5:2-7).

Consider this wayward nation and rebellious people: they had been cared for, planted, and cultivated by the very hand of God, but they produced only bad fruit—just like the fig tree that Jesus cursed when it bore no fruit, only leaves. This vineyard, then, is the house of Israel—God's choice vine, the garden of His delight—but it is spoiled. And so God says, "I will remove its protection, and briers and thorns will grow." Briers and thorns are the very sign of the curse, the sign of de-creation. Good things being turned into a desert is what happens when men rebel against God. The cursed ground produced thorns and thistles, and God's vineyard was turned into a wilderness.

The Blood of Grapes

In the forty-ninth chapter of Genesis we read how Jacob blessed his sons. He goes through the tribes, pronouncing the blessing of God upon them. He comes to Judah, and to Judah (whose name means "praise") he says:

> *Judah, your brothers will praise you; your hand will be on the neck of your enemies; your father's sons will bow down to you. You are a lion's cub, O Judah; you return from the prey, my son. Like a lion he crouches and lies down, like a lioness—who dares to rouse him? The scepter will not depart from Judah, nor the ruler's staff from between his feet, until he comes to whom it belongs and the obedience of the nations is his. He will tether his donkey to a vine, his colt to the choicest branch; he will wash his garments in wine, his robes in the blood of grapes. His eyes will be darker than wine, his teeth whiter than milk* (Genesis 49:8-12).

Now this first mention of anyone having his or her robes stained with blood is spoken of as a blessing upon Judah. And, of course, all things that are spoken to Judah find their ultimate fulfillment in Jesus, for He is the one who holds the scepter, who rules over the nations with a rod of iron, and it is to Him their obedience is due. But it is spoken of here as a prophetic picture of someone who washes His robes in wine, in the blood of grapes. There is no concept or idea of punishment here. There is no suggestion of wrath. It is just a statement, and I believe that the statement is communicating this: Judah is going to be such a fruitful vine, overflowing with such abundance, that wine will be as common as water. There will be so much wine that it will be as if he could wash his garments in the wine. Where other people would use water, he would use wine.

Remember Jesus' first miracle. At the wedding in Cana of Galilee, there were six stone water pots that were used for the

Jewish custom of purification, for washing. The Jews were obsessive washers. They washed their hands, their feet, and their faces. They washed every new pot and utensil that they bought. There was an obsession with washing, and it was all to do with outward religion, with outward cleanliness. And Jesus used these stone water pots that held between 20 and 30 gallons each. They were not little jugs; these were huge oil-drum sized things filled with water. He had them filled to the brim. This point is very carefully recorded. They are filled to the brim because it is out of His fullness that we receive from Him. Out of the fullness of water comes the wine of the Kingdom.

Jesus made wine as plentiful as water, and that is what is prophesied about Judah. He is going to have so much wine that he is going to do his laundry in it! Wine will be as common as water. But the picture is dramatic because washing one's clothes in wine would stain them. This is a picture that the prophets will build on. What we need to see at this point is that there is no concept of wrath or judgment yet. It is just speaking of the bounty and the overflowing blessing that belongs to Judah.

However, let us look at another passage where garments are described as being washed in the blood of the grape.

> *Who is this coming from Edom, from Bozrah, with His garments stained crimson? Who is this, robed in splendor, striding forward in the greatness of His strength? "It is I, speaking in righteousness, mighty to save." Why are Your garments red, like those of one treading the winepress? "I have trodden the winepress alone; from the nations no one was with Me. I trampled them in My anger and trod them down in My wrath; their blood spattered*

> *My garments, and I stained all My clothing. For the day of vengeance was in My heart, and the year of My redemption has come. I looked, but there was no one to help, I was appalled that no one gave support; so My own arm worked salvation for Me, and My own wrath sustained Me. I trampled the nations in My anger; in My wrath I made them drunk and poured their blood on the ground"* (Isaiah 63:1-6).

Now there are some apparent contradictions here, for the Lord is coming in glory and splendor, and He is coming in wrath and anger. He is coming to judge and trample the nations, but He is the Lord who is mighty to save. Not only is He mighty to save, but He has come because the day of vengeance had arrived. Now we are back into a scenario that tells us that what for one is bloodshed, horror, and death, for another is redemption and salvation. In other words, the winepress is the place where your destiny is decided.

The Winepress

Let me pursue this a little further. I have stated that the sign of the new world into which Noah emerged was a vineyard. The sign of the new land that God brought His people into was a vineyard. And the sign of the church, of course, is a vineyard. Jesus said, *"I am the vine; you are the branches"* (John 15:5). So God uses this vineyard image to portray His purposes at different times throughout history. But His purpose has always been the same: to have a vineyard over which He cares and that produces the new wine of the Kingdom so that it will flow and satisfy the hearts of men and women (see Joel 3:18). Yet in the two passages that we read in the Book of

Revelation, we see in it something of a context of judgment. The idea comes from the third chapter of Joel, as so much does in the Book of Revelation. Here it says:

> *Swing the sickle, for the harvest is ripe. Come, trample the grapes, for the winepress is full and the vats overflow—so great is their wickedness!* (Joel 3:13)

God is going to trample a rebellious world, and yet the trampling of the winepress, which is death to the rebellious, is going to be life for us, because there is a sense in which Jesus not only trampled the grapes in the winepress, but Jesus Himself was trampled in the winepress. If we acknowledge that Jesus was trampled on our behalf, then we are redeemed. If we refuse to respond to His vicarious suffering, then we will be lost, and we ourselves will be those who are trampled. By the way, trampling in Scripture is always a demonstration of God's utter rejection. Remember we saw that the outer court of the temple would be trampled because God was rejecting it. Jesus said that if salt loses its flavor—if the covenant people do not live like covenant people, if they do not pervade their society with the preserving influence of the Kingdom of God, if they forsake Him—it is good for nothing but to be cast out and trampled under the feet of men (see Matt. 5:13). It is utterly rejected and useless.

Let me take you back to chapter 14 of Revelation, where we see Jesus treading the grapes of wrath, and we are told,

> *The angel swung his sickle on the earth, gathered its grapes and threw them into the great winepress of God's wrath. They were trampled in the winepress outside the city, and blood flowed out of the press, rising as high as*

> *the horses' bridles for a distance of 1,600 stadia* (Revelation 14:19-20).

There are three things that are important for us to notice here.

Outside the City

First, the winepress is outside the city. This immediately reminds us that this is not just where God's wrath was poured out on the nations, but it is where God's wrath fell on His Son. The writer to the Hebrews tells us, "*Jesus also suffered outside the city gate to make the people holy through His own blood. Let us, then, go to Him outside the camp, bearing the disgrace He bore*" (Heb. 13:12-13). He is saying, "Jesus suffered, He was crushed and trampled in the winepress, to make His people holy by His blood." This blood is not just the blood of vengeance, nor is it the blood of those who have been destroyed through their rebellion. It is also the blood of Jesus, because He suffered outside the gate, outside the city.

1,600 Stadia

Christ was crushed in God's winepress of judgment, and He released His blood as a healing and cleansing flow for the whole world. For this blood, Scripture tells us, flowed out for a vast distance—1,600 stadia, which is about 200 miles. But the main point of this figure is that 1,600 is 40 times 40, which is the period of probation, the period of waiting. There was a waiting of 40 years in the wilderness. There were 40 days of rain during the flood and 40 days of waiting before Noah disembarked. For 40 days Jesus was tempted by the devil. Forty represents the days of probation or days of testing. God gives 40 times 40 periods for men to come to repentance and faith.

Not only does 1,600 represent time, but it also represents place: it is 4 × 4 × 100. The number four has to do with the earth, the whole earth. In a similar way in which we have seen 12 × 12 × 1000 describes the entire redeemed community, we now find that 4 × 4 × 100 (100 being another full and rounded number) signifying the whole world. This figure is expanding our understanding that God is concerned about the whole world and that the blood is effective for every nation under Heaven.

The Bridles of the Horses

We also need to notice the strange remark about the blood: it came up to the bridle of the horses. What is the significance of this odd detail? It is telling us not only that it must be fairly deep, but that the blood of Jesus has produced a new Red Sea in which the horses of the rebellious are overflowed and destroyed. In fact, when you go into the next chapter of Revelation, to the verses that immediately follow this image, you find the scene that we looked at in a previous chapter, in which the great redeemed community is standing around the sea of glass that has fire mixed in it and that looks like another Red Sea. So we are looking again at the Exodus paradigm, the crossing of the Red Sea, the redemption of God's people.

The prophet Zechariah speaks of a time when all the nations will flow to Jerusalem to worship God. There will be such a move of redemption that the good news will affect every nation under Heaven, and there will be an incredible response as they come and worship God. What is more, he says, they will come and worship God at a specific time. It will be at the Feast of

Tabernacles (see Zech. 14:16). Now of the three feasts that God gave Israel to commemorate the Exodus every year, the Feast of Tabernacles is the only one that has not yet been fulfilled in terms of its prophetic significance. Passover has been fulfilled by Christ our Lamb, who has been sacrificed. The Day of Pentecost has been fulfilled by the coming of the Holy Spirit. But Tabernacles began when the final stage of harvest—the gathering of the grapes—was completed. It was for Israel the ultimate harvest, the ingathering. It has not yet come, but the fourteenth chapter of Zechariah is a picture of the ultimate harvest, the harvest festival and celebration of the great ingathering from the earth of all men and tribes and nations and peoples.

Zechariah says that the world is going to come up and worship God at the Feast of Tabernacles. At this festival they commemorated many things, but the main thing was God's care for them in the wilderness where they lived in tents, or tabernacles. So what they had to do was to gather the green, leafy, and fruitful boughs of many trees, make themselves little huts, and then live in them for a week. They came to Jerusalem to celebrate the festival, so in Jerusalem, on every street and in every courtyard, in every empty space, and on every roof there would be little green boughs, little cabins or huts, little refuges of green and leafy boughs, full of fruit and fragrance, where the people would come and live. Approaching Jerusalem from a distance, it would look as if the mountain of the Lord had been turned into a garden. Paradise had been restored.

One of the conflicts throughout Scripture is that between Zion and Babylon. And Babylon actually was one of the wonders of the world because of its hanging gardens. Babylon was not only a false city and a false mountain, it was also a false garden. It was the place of ultimate falsehood and unrighteousness

And, says Zechariah, when the nations come to celebrate the Feast of Tabernacles, righteousness will be so abounding that "holiness to the Lord," that seal that is over the forehead of the priest of God, will be written on the bells of the horses (see Zech. 14:20). So this Red Sea of blood that covers the world not only destroys the horses of Pharaoh's army, but it sanctifies everything else so that even horses, when the blood comes up to their bridles where their bells dangle, will have "holy to the Lord" written on them. This sea of blood is therefore a sanctifying stream.

It is a destroying flood, but it is also a sanctifying stream. How we enter and come out of the river, or of the sea, depends on our relationship to Jesus. It is a time of judgment but also a time of deliverance. It is death to Pharaoh's horse but "holy to the Lord" for your horse. It is the end of nations that rebel, but it is the birth of the nation that will obey. This is God's plan and God's purpose, and we do not need to fear the vengeance of God in the winepress, for one in the winepress has already carried the vengeance of God in His own body. We do not have to fear the judgment of God to break upon us, for one who was completely pure and holy has borne that judgment for us. We do not have to fear the stripes of God, for one has borne the stripes in the winepress. Why are His robes stained with blood? Because Jesus trod the winepress for us. There is a time coming when judgment will break on our earth; but we have been judged already; judged and found not guilty because our faith is in Jesus Christ.

CHAPTER 8

Babylon Fallen, Part 1

We will begin this chapter by returning to the 144,000 we considered earlier. You will need to read Revelation 14:1-8. As you read, it should not surprise you that when you see the redeemed community in worship before the Lamb on Mount Zion, in the same context you read that Babylon is falling. For there is constant conflict between Babylon and Zion, and as Zion emerges so Babylon falls.

A Tale of Two Cities

The opening chapters of the Bible are very important for us because they reveal to us the essence of everything that God is going to say from this moment on and indicate everything that the Spirit of God wants to achieve. When we come to chapter

11 in the Book of Genesis, we read that men sought to build a city for themselves, and it notes: "*As men moved eastward, they found a plain*" (Gen. 11:2). Now everything in God's creation teaches us something about God. When Adam sinned, he was cast out of the garden eastward. When Cain killed his brother, he went from the presence of the Lord eastward. After the Flood and the beginning of the repopulation of the world, men traveled eastward. This idea of moving eastward conveys to us a departure from God. It is symbolic. It does not mean that people who live in the East are more sinful than those in the West, because the simple fact is that we all live east of somebody else! But in the Bible eastward represents a departure from God. That is why, whenever the tabernacle was erected and when the temple was built, their doorways faced the east, which means you have to turn around from the way you were going by nature and come back to God. If you look at a map in the back of your Bible and find Ur of the Chaldeans from which Abraham came, you will notice that his pilgrimage took him from the east to the west. That is also why when Jesus came into the world, wise men from the East came to worship Him. God is showing us that He is calling the world to turn around from its headlong departure from His presence and come to seek Him again.

And here we find men traveling east, and as they travel, they come to a plain. It is upon this plain that they want to build their city. Of course, we have already noted many times that Zion is a hill and that the holy city of God is built on a hill, not on a plain. It is much easier to build a city on a plain than it is to build a city on a hill. So sinful men take the easy option and say: "*Come, let us build ourselves a city, with a tower that reaches to the heavens, so that we may make a name for ourselves*" (Gen. 11:4).

We, on the other hand, are looking for a city that comes down out of Heaven. Arrogant humanism believes it can build a city that will elevate man up into the heavens so that men become gods. It is not at all without significance that it is in this eleventh chapter that we are first introduced to Abraham. Right at the beginning of the Bible we see a conflict of ideals. There are those who are eastbound plain dwellers who want to make a name for themselves and who intend to ascend into the heavens by their own efforts. They are contrasted with a man who has left a city, a highly fortified and sophisticated city, because he has seen a city of infinitely greater value. He has seen the City of God, "which has foundations," whose builder and maker is not these eastward travelers but God (see Heb. 11:8-10). He is looking for a city that comes down out of Heaven from God. He is not looking for a city built of man-made bricks, but he is looking for a city that is constructed with living stones. Right at the beginning we find this conflict of concepts and ideologies.

This conflict is developed all the way through the Scriptures. Babylon, which has its beginning in the Tower of Babel, is the place that stands opposed to the things of God. It is a humanistic alternative to God's spiritual reality. But it is destined to fall. Everything it stands for is destined to collapse. As Zion arises, Babylon crumbles. In fact, when we look in chapter 16 of Revelation and see the outpouring of the bowls of wrath, it is the final outpouring that actually begins the end of Babylon:

> *The seventh angel poured out his bowl into the air, and out of the temple came a loud voice from the throne, saying, "It is done!" Then there came flashes of lightning, rumblings, peals of thunder and a severe earthquake. No earthquake like it has ever occurred since man has been*

> *on earth, so tremendous was the quake. The great city split into three parts, and the cities of the nations collapsed. God remembered Babylon the Great and gave her the cup filled with the wine of the fury of His wrath. Every island fled away and the mountains could not be found. From the sky huge hailstones of about a hundred pounds each fell upon men. And they cursed God on account of the plague of hail, because the plague was so terrible* (Revelation 16:17-21).

God's judgment is coming upon everything that is of Babylon, but because she is so fixed in her hostility, so determined to pursue her rebellion rather than repent and call for mercy, she curses God. We live in an arrogant world where people will curse God without any fear. But their retribution is at hand. God will not let the world go unpunished. Chapters 17 and 18 are all about the fall of Babylon. It gets huge coverage in the Book of Revelation because ultimately this is what the Book of Revelation is about—the triumph of the God of Zion over Babylon.

Babylon Is Jerusalem!

The very sobering thing, however, is that what John calls Babylon here is actually what was historically known as Jerusalem. The covenant-breaking people, who were chosen to display the glory of God, have now rejected their king. They have said, "*Let His blood be on us and on our children!*" (Matt. 27:25). They have cried, "*We have no king but Caesar*" (John 19:15), so now their fig tree has withered, their house is left to them desolate, and all that is left to occur is the pouring out of God's wrath on these unbelieving and ungrateful sons. Jerusalem has become Babylon.

Let me explain why I believe that this is so. Babylon is described in the Book of Revelation as the great prostitute. Now that is the accusation that is continually made by the prophets of God not to the world, not to the heathen nations, and not to those who are locked in pagan darkness, but to God's own people. The accusation of adultery and of prostitution is made not to the Gentiles but to Jerusalem.

This is a constant and recurring theme, but because it may be new to some readers and controversial to others, let us look at several Scriptures. We will start with the prophet Isaiah:

> *See how the faithful city has become a harlot! She once was full of justice; righteousness used to dwell in her—but now murderers! Your silver has become dross, your choice wine is diluted with water. Your rulers are rebels, companions of thieves; they all love bribes and chase after gifts. They do not defend the cause of the fatherless; the widow's case does not come before them* (Isaiah 1:21-23).

The faithful city has become a prostitute. That is the prophetic accusation against Jerusalem.

> *Long ago you broke off your yoke and tore off your bonds; you said, "I will not serve You!" Indeed, on every high hill and under every spreading tree you lay down as a prostitute. I had planted you like a choice vine of sound and reliable stock. How then did you turn against Me into a corrupt, wild vine?* (Jeremiah 2:20-21)

How has she become corrupt? She is lying down and is opening her legs for everybody! She is wanton and rebellious.

> *This is your lot, the portion I have decreed for you," declares the Lord, "because you have forgotten Me and trusted in false gods. I will pull up your skirts over your face that your shame may be seen—your adulteries and lustful neighings, your shameless prostitution! I have seen your detestable acts on the hills and in the fields. Woe to you, O Jerusalem! How long will you be unclean?* (Jeremiah 13:25-27).

These are serious accusations. These are awesome and awful words. The faithful city, the pure bride, the one whom God betrothed himself to, has turned into a wanton prostitute. In fact, if we were to search all the Scriptures we could almost compile a whole book of the accusations that God makes, for not only is she the prostitute who loves the wages of her prostitution, she actually pays lovers to come and defile her. This is what God says about this city. So when we find, in the Book of Revelation, that there are accusations against a city that is full of prostitution and in fact has become a prostitute, we know that that was the very accusation that all the prophets carried about the Jerusalem of God.

The fullest and most appalling description of Israel's prostitution and adultery is found in the twenty-third chapter of Book of Ezekiel. The prophet speaks of the two kingdoms, the Northern Kingdom, which comprised ten tribes, and the Southern Kingdom, which was called Judah but was actually the two tribes of Benjamin and Judah. He tells how the Northern Kingdom vanished after it was captured, overcome, and exiled by the Assyrians. Then he goes on to speak of the

Southern Kingdom, which is later in the Scriptures called Judea, whose capital was Jerusalem; and this Southern Kingdom carries her prostitution even further than the Northern Kingdom. It is not a pleasant read and is the kind of passage you quickly pass over in your quiet time! It is not the stuff for Sunday School. It is embarrassing just to read it. We feel uncomfortable listening to the words, but this is God's word.

It raises the question as to why some Christians believe that God has reserved natural Israel in special favor when she has defiled and betrayed him so wantonly. She is the prostitute. Israel of today, when they worship God, are not worshiping the God we worship. They are worshiping a god of their own imagination, of their own invention. Modern Judaism is not the religion of Old Testament: it is prostitution. So when John speaks of the mother of harlots, he is not speaking of natural Babylon. He is not speaking of natural Rome. He is speaking of Jerusalem! How sad! How awful! But we should not be surprised, because the descriptions of her harlotry have filled the books of the prophets. The terrible descriptions that they give, the detail that they recount, is embarrassing and shocking. We would rather not read it. We would rather close our eyes and pretend it was not there—but it is there, and it is there to tell us that those people who reject God have taken on the very nature of the worst kind of prostitution.

The Prophet Hosea

Let us consider the prophet Hosea. One of the things that prophets have to do is to feel what God feels. We have to know how God feels because, for example, it is the love of Christ that constrains us. We therefore have to feel what Christ feels.

If Christ feels great love, then it is only as we feel great love that we are motivated to do the work that Christ calls us to do. We have to identify with God, not only theologically but emotionally. And Hosea has to enter into the heartache of God. God calls him to marry a prostitute. Of course, if he were in your church, he would be out of it in double quick time! But he is doing it in obedience to the word of God. He is enacting and experiencing a prophetic drama. He is not just saying he will pick up some girl on the street corner and go through some kind of Las Vegas marriage with her that does not mean anything. It would not have worked like that. He went and married a prostitute, and the Bible makes it very clear that he loved her. His feelings had to be touched. He had to be totally involved. He could not just act.

> *When the Lord began to speak through Hosea, the Lord said to him, "Go, take to yourself an adulterous wife and children of unfaithfulness, because the land is guilty of the vilest adultery in departing from the Lord"* (Hosea 1:2-3).

And then we need to read on into the second chapter:

> *Rebuke your mother, rebuke her, for she is not My wife, and I am not her husband. Let her remove the adulterous look from her face and the unfaithfulness from between her breasts. Otherwise I will strip her naked and make her as bare as on the day she was born; I will make her like a desert, turn her into a parched land, and slay her with thirst. I will not show My love to her children, because they are the children of adultery. Their mother has been unfaithful and has conceived them in disgrace. She said, "I will go after my lovers, who give me my food and my*

> *water, my wool and my linen, my oil and my drink." Therefore I will block her path with thornbushes; I will wall her in so that she cannot find her way. She will chase after her lovers but not catch them; she will look for them but not find them. Then she will say, "I will go back to my husband as at first, for then I was better off than now." She has not acknowledged that I was the one who gave her the grain, the new wine and oil, who lavished on her the silver and gold—which they used for Baal* (Hosea 2:1-8).

This is a remarkable history of adultery, prostitution, and unfaithfulness. What does John say happened when their own king came, when their true husband arrived? *"He came to that which was His own, but His own did not receive Him"* (John 1:11). They were given to another. They belonged, they claimed, to Caesar and had no king but him. Therefore, they were going to inherit the wages of their prostitution. Listen to what Hosea says again:

> *Do not rejoice, O Israel; do not be jubilant like the other nations. For you have been unfaithful to your God; you love the wages of a prostitute at every threshing floor* (Hosea 9:1).

Now I apologize for taking so much time to make this one point, but I have not exhausted the Scriptures by any means that speak in this way. What we need to understand is that God had an ongoing problem with the faithfulness of His people. You will be aware of the many times that they forsook him, when they turned away from Him and began to worship other gods, and in the Scriptures, particularly in the prophets, idolatry is identical to adultery. For when they worshiped other gods, it was as if they were betraying their husband in an adulterous relationship. That is the history of Jerusalem.

Of course, because Jerusalem is being likened to Babylon, we find historic references to Babylon that are now applied to Jerusalem. For instance, we see the prostitute come riding out on a red beast, and she is the one described as sitting on many waters. Back in Jeremiah that is how Babylon is described, the city by many waters (see Rev. 17:1,15). But we have already seen that in the Book of Revelation waters represent peoples, the restless heathens, the rebellious nations; Babylon is exerting her influence over the nations. With her, the Scripture says, the kings of the earth committed adultery. This is the great accusation of the prophets to Israel. Not only that, but Paul claims that God's name was blasphemed among the Gentiles because of Israel's apostasy (see Rom. 2:24).

So this is not just an historic event that has all been patched up. This is not a breakdown in a relationship that has gone to marriage guidance counseling and been all sorted out. This is an ongoing and a recurring habit that Jerusalem has had of betraying the faithfulness and trust of God. In Jesus' day and generation He looked at those who were alive at that time. Now He was not speaking historically, He was speaking to those alive at that time when He said, "You are an adulterous generation" (e.g., Matt. 16:4). This is not just an insult. He has not just lost His temper and not been able to think of a better swear word to use! He is actually describing the spiritual attitude of the people among whom He has come, a people who reject Him, who will not receive Him, and who determine in their hearts actually to murder Him.

There was a conspiracy between the harlot and the beast upon which she rode, for the prostitute rode upon the political power of her day. The apostate religion rode upon the political tyrant to get her own way. Read the Acts of the Apostles again and just make a mark every time that it tells you that the Jews complained to the Romans about the Christians and provoked the Romans to act against the Christians. What is happening? The prostitute is riding the beast to persecute the saints! That should not surprise us, because that is exactly what happened when they crucified Jesus. They came and complained to the Romans, who told them to deal with it, but they responded by saying that they could not inflict the death penalty, so they insisted that the Romans do it. The prostitute guided the beast to this terrible conclusion, but it was all in the plan and the purpose of God.

These things are not difficult to discover. Throughout the Word of God we see where the harlot has intoxicated the world with her wine. The prophet Jeremiah said, "*Babylon was a gold cup in the Lord's hand; she made the whole earth drunk. The nations drank her wine; therefore they have now gone mad*" (Jer. 51:7). The Book of Revelation echoes, "*All the nations drink the maddening wine of her adulteries*" (Rev. 14:8). Remember the persecution that came on the church in the second and third chapters of Revelation, where Jesus wrote to the churches. He spoke of those who said they were Jews and were not. He spoke of the place where the synagogue of satan is. They are not Jews anymore. They are prostitutes. They are not the sons of God anymore. They are of their father, the devil.

> *Then the angel carried me away in the Spirit into a desert. There I saw a woman sitting on a scarlet beast*

that was covered with blasphemous names and had seven heads and ten horns. The woman was dressed in purple and scarlet, and was glittering with gold, precious stones and pearls (Revelation 17:3-4).

I do not have any firsthand experience of this, and I am sure none of you do either, but if a prostitute is successfully going to ply her trade, she is not going to get very far if she looks like the back of a bus. She has got to be glamorous. At least she has got to have some kind of surface glamour, some kind of attraction. The problem with deception is that it is very attractive. It does not work otherwise. The problem with the prostitute is that she looks all right, but she is all wrong. She is a phony and a fraud. But she has yet to be unmasked, and right now she looks pretty good. That is why when John sees her he is amazed. She is not a wizened old hag with warts. She is an incredible-looking creature.

She could be a contender for Miss World, but she is bad news and, as John looks, he notices that she has a name written on her forehead. Now that should not surprise us. We have found that throughout this book. Those who stand on Mount Zion and worship the Lamb have His name and His Father's name on their foreheads. But this women has something else written on her forehead:

MYSTERY
BABYLON THE GREAT
THE MOTHER OF PROSTITUTES
AND OF THE ABOMINATIONS OF THE EARTH
(Revelation 17:5).

This is a foul parody of the holy priesthood, of the man who stood in robes of righteousness in the presence of God, who worshiped in the beauty of holiness, who came and gave himself on behalf of the people to the worship and the work of God, and who had "Holy to the Lord" written upon his forehead. Here comes a whore in a blasphemous act of worship, blatantly displaying her corruption and wearing on her head a sign that marks her out as a worshiper of the beast.

She is the prostitute. She is the mystery. There are many mysteries in Scripture, and a mystery in the Bible is just a truth that you have not seen yet. That is all it is. Much of the New Testament is about unveiling mysteries. The Book of Revelation is about unveiling a mystery, and Paul speaks about the mystery of iniquity that is at work at this present time (see 2 Thess. 2:7). The mystery of Babylon is still real. It is still happening. It is still out there. And just as the Book of Revelation is an unveiling of Jesus, it is an unmasking of the devil. Just as it is a revelation of Him who is the holy Lamb of God, it is also an exposure of her who rides upon the beast. We need to know who is who and what is what. We need to know not that which is attractive and appeals to the senses, but that which is true and calls to the spirit.

When Israel was coming into the land of promise to inhabit the land and bring in the kingdom, their first great success was Jericho, where, by the seven horns of the anointed lamb, the walls fell down. Their great failure was Ai, and the reason they failed at Ai, or one of the reasons they failed at Ai, is because a man found a gorgeous, beautiful, and enticing Babylonian garment that he hid in his tent. Right from the beginning Babylon has been seeking to divert the people of God. Babylon had been seeking to deceive the people of God, and it is still at work today. Are we going to trust the Lamb, or are we going to ride the beast? Well, we now know what our choice is, but we need our eyes open to see what is happening in our world and in our church in these days.

CHAPTER 9

Babylon Fallen, Part 2

John gives more than two chapters to the destruction of Babylon, which should impress us with the enormity of what it is referring to. It conveys to us that what John is dealing with is no passing affliction with a quick-fix solution but something of extreme importance. He goes into great detail about the destruction of this prostitute city. He claims that the sinful influence of this city has corrupted the whole world. It is interesting to note that the Jews had been dispersed to all the nations of the Empire. Their influence was felt in every nation; in fact, as you read in the Acts of the Apostles, in every nation they became the instigators of the attacks against the Christians. Paul says that the name of God is blasphemed among all the nations because of their apostasy and their false testimony that they bear to the covenant of

God. The Jews were spread far and wide. Jesus said to the Pharisees, "*You travel over land and sea to win a single convert, and when he becomes one, you make him twice as much a son of hell as you are*" (Matt. 23:15). There was clearly a Judaistic influence throughout the Roman Empire and in all the cities where the Gospel was to be preached.

It is true that Paul always went first to the Jews, and Jews became the first fruits of his Gospel endeavors in the city. He went to the synagogue and preached the good news of the Kingdom. We invariably find, however, that, somewhere along the line, the Jews refused to listen. Eventually, he takes those converts that he has made and sets up his operation in some other part of the city. He was living in perpetual pressure from the opposition of the religious leaders.

Initially, then, Babylon stands for Jerusalem, but it also represents everything that is not of Christ; it is anti-Christ. Everything that is not the bride is a prostitute. Everything that is not true Zion is Babylon. Babylon is bigger than just Jerusalem. Babylon embraces in its adulterous arms everything that stands against Jesus and the knowledge of His glory. Therefore, humanism, "Christian" heresies, and other religions are all incorporated into the Babylonian concept that Scripture communicates to us. First, it is Jerusalem because she is the harlot and the adulteress. But everyone who takes a stand with her, who compromises with her, comes into an adulterous lifestyle. Remember when Jesus addressed the churches, and He confronted some of them with the peril in which they stood because of the compromise they were making with the world. One of the accusations He made was of the woman Jezebel. Whether there was actually a woman in that church with that actual name is irrelevant. What He is doing is identifying her with the terrible prostitute queen who was married to King Ahab and who seduced the whole nation to follow a false religion. He is saying she is just like her and, having identified her, He also identifies what she does. She teaches them to eat food offered to idols and to indulge in sexual immorality. And that is what those who held to the teaching of Balaam did.

Do you remember Balaam, who was hired by Abimelech to curse Israel but could not do it? That is our confidence: no one can curse us, because we are the people of God. If we are in the blessing of God, there is nowhere for a curse to land. That is actually the words of the writer of the Proverbs, who says that an undeserved curse is like a fluttering bird. It cannot find anywhere to land (see Prov. 26:2). They can send it out, but it cannot land on you. When Balaam discovered that he could not curse them, he encouraged the king to seduce them. He sent women among them to persuade them to eat meat offered to idols and to commit adultery.

What we are seeing here is the ultimate collapse of Israel, who was meant to be the wife of God but who has become a prostitute. Prophetically, however, we are seeing the collapse of everything that stands against God, everything that will not submit to Him and bring its glory into His city.

The Prostitute and the Beast

Now one of the interesting things about this woman is that she is in league with the beast, and yet in the end it is the beast who is going to destroy her. Jesus said, when He was accused of casting out demons by the power of satan, "*A house divided against itself will fall"* (Luke 11:17). The truth about the house of satan is that it is divided. There is not one clear agenda or one cohesive aim. There is not one demonic fellowship that has its eye on an ultimate goal. Everybody is out for himself or herself. That is what it is like to be in the kingdom of darkness. It is to do your own thing. When we saw those terrible locusts issuing from the abyss, every single one of them wore a crown because, although they have a king—which natural locusts do not (see Prov. 30:27)—every one of them was the boss of his own life. That is the kind of society in which we live today. That is what the pit has spawned: individualism to the extreme, individualism that revolves around what I want and what is good for me. There is no moral standard. There is no socially accepted behavior. Whatever you want goes. That is the sign of a society that has lost the concept of responsibility. We live in an age when everyone has rights and no one has responsibilities. That is Babylon.

One of the things we discover about Babylon when she falls is that it causes worldwide consternation. Everyone is upset—not because they have sympathy for her, but because their own livelihood is now under threat. All the kings, the merchants, and the ship owners are in deep mourning and distress because of Babylon's fall—not because they care for Babylon, not because their heart goes out to her in her time of trial, but because they have suddenly lost their profit. This is a society that needs to fall. It has no compassion. It does not care. It does not look after the fatherless. It does not support the widow. Everyone is out for himself or herself. And let us note this:

> *When the kings of the earth who committed adultery with her and shared her luxury see the smoke of her burning, they will weep and mourn over her. Terrified at her torment, they will stand far off* (Revelation 18:9-10a).

I would have thought in a time of such terror, turmoil, and need, you would want someone who would support you, comfort you, put an arm around you. But as they see her torment they stand far off, they distance themselves. They are concerned because their profit margins have suddenly been drastically reduced.

> *Terrified at her torment, they will stand far off and cry: "Woe! Woe, O great city, O Babylon, city of power! In one hour your doom has come!" The merchants of the earth will weep and mourn over her because no one buys their cargoes any more—cargoes of gold, silver, precious stones and pearls; fine linen, purple, silk and scarlet cloth; every sort of citron wood, and articles of every kind made of ivory, costly wood, bronze, iron and marble; cargoes of cinnamon and spice, of incense, myrrh and frankincense, of wine and olive oil, of fine flour and wheat; cattle and sheep; horses and carriages; and bodies and souls of men* (Revelation 18:10-13).

That is the stock in trade of Babylon. It trades in the bodies and souls of men. Babylon, true to her nature, is a slave trader. She captivates, captures, and incarcerates men. Babylon not only captures their bodies, but their souls. She not only sells them into slavery, she sells them into deception and despair, into lies and error and ultimately into death. What a wicked city. What an awful place. What a happy moment that she should collapse and her smoke go up forever. God has treated her in exactly the same way as he treated Sodom. The smoke of her destruction goes up forever and ever, and all the things that she once delighted in have suddenly, in one hour, come to an end. God, when He determines to move, can move very swiftly. In one hour He destroys her, brings her to nothing, to devastation. That is terrible news for the godless but great news for the righteous—that God can move swiftly.

In the Old Testament a prophet had asked a rhetorical question, one that demands an affirmative answer. The rhetorical question was this: Can a nation be born in a day? (see Isa. 66:8). Well, yes—and a nation can be brought to nothing in an hour. A city can be laid bare in a moment. Destruction can come upon them suddenly, and, if God can pull down the empires of this world, if God can destroy the principalities that have influence over our world in a moment of time, God can bring forth His purpose, manifest His people, and demonstrate His glory quicker than our imagination can grasp. When God moves by His Spirit he can achieve more in a moment than our strategy will achieve in a lifetime. That is why we call on God to move. We cannot go out and pull down Babylon. But God, in a moment, can destroy everything that stands against Him. God will use to His own ends those who are actually opposed to Him. God will use those who are His enemies to destroy His enemies. God will use, like some divine puppeteer, everything that will blaspheme and rile against His name and holiness and make it fulfill His purpose.

You see, the prostitute burdens the beast. She is riding on him to bring destruction to humanity. This is another of those dreadful parodies of a humble King riding into Jerusalem on a donkey, who came to bring redemption and deliverance, a humble king who was greeted by the cries and the shouts and the hosannas of the multitude, of people who laid down their clothes before Him as a drama of how their very lives would be brought into submission to His lordship. But in a moment their cry was changed to "Crucify him! Away with him! We will not have this man to reign over us!" (see Matt. 27:22; Luke 19:14; 23:18). Jesus came humble and riding on a donkey, and instead of receiving the King on the donkey, they welcomed the prostitute on a beast. Instead of welcoming Him whose name is King of Kings and Lord of Lords, they welcomed her whose name was Mother of Prostitutes and of the Abominations of the Earth. They got what they deserved.

Do you remember that we heard the altar respond to an angelic cry, that when God had turned the waters into blood, the angel said, "*They have shed the blood of Your saints and prophets, and You have given them blood to drink as they deserve*" (Rev. 16:6). God will always give you what you deserve. When He comes to apportion prize or punishment, it is always what you deserve. That is nothing to do with salvation. Salvation is getting what you do not deserve, but reward is getting what you do deserve. Retribution is getting what you deserve, and Jerusalem received what she deserved. Babylon is visited by God's retribution in utter justice, for the beast itself attacks the woman. It strips her bare, eats her up, and burns her with fire.

It is like Jezebel again. Jezebel dealt in the souls of men and sold them to demonic powers that were exercised through the prophets of Baal. When God came to deal with her, she was cast down, literally, out of a window, smashed on the ground. And the dogs ate her. Beasts devoured her; the prostitute was eaten by a monster. The monster that she was once in partnership with, on whose back she once rode, whom she urged on to persecute the people of God will now turn on her and eat her up. We do not have to fight against Babylon. Babylon will destroy itself.

Come Out and Be Separate

There is another cry in Heaven:

> *Then I heard another voice from Heaven say: "Come out of her, My people, so that you will not share in her sins, so that you will not receive any of her plagues; for her sins are piled up to Heaven, and God has remembered her crimes"* (Revelation 18:4-5).

Notice how God describes her sins—they are piled up to Heaven. That is how Paul, by the way, speaks about the Jews:

> *For you, brothers, became imitators of God's churches in Judea, which are in Christ Jesus: You suffered from your own countrymen the same things those churches suffered from the Jews, who killed the Lord Jesus and the prophets and also drove us out. They displease God and are hostile to all men in their effort to keep us from speaking to the Gentiles so that they may be saved. In this way they always heap up their sins to the limit. The wrath of God has come upon them at last* (1 Thessalonians 2:14-16).

God says Israel, in its hostility to the Church and to Jesus, in its murder of the prophets and its rejection of the apostles, has piled up its sins to the limit, and when it reaches the limit, God's wrath comes upon them at last. And when Babylon's sins are piled up to the limit, God retaliates. He says, "You have reached the limit!" Remember that Abraham's offspring came into Canaan when the Amorites had filled up the fullness of their sins. So when Babylon's sins are fulfilled, Babylon falls; but as Babylon falls, Zion emerges. Jesus said something almost identical to this.

> *So you testify against yourselves that you are the descendants of those who murdered the prophets. Fill up, then, the measure of the sin of your forefathers!* (Matthew 23:31-32)

In chapter 18 of Revelation, that is exactly what we see them do. They fill up the sin of their forefathers. They fill it up to the limit, and God's wrath comes upon them at last, for the harlot's sins have reached up to the heavens, and God has responded. But God knows those who are His, and God knows how to rescue the righteous (see Isa. 48:20; Jer. 50:8; 51:6,9,45; 2 Cor. 6:17; Rev. 18:4;). So God sends a call, an alarm, a challenge: "Come out of her, My people!" Now the amazing thing is that there are genuine people of God, true saints, born-again men and women, who are in Babylon. God will not utterly destroy Babylon and bring it to an end until his people have come out of her. He does not want them to share in her sin. He does not want them to be affected by her plagues. A very obvious and current situation to compare this to is the homosexual issue in many denominational churches. Such churches have compromised with Babylon and have been infected by her spirit: "*A little yeast works through the whole batch of dough*" (1 Cor. 5:6). Because of this and a multitude of other issues, it's time for real believers to separate themselves. He wants to bring everything that is Babylon to an end, but He will not do it while you are there. This is a strange thing for those of us who believe in a sovereign God, who believe that the King will do as He desires and none can withstand Him. But there is a sense in which God has bound Himself in partnership with us. God has limited Himself to our response. Now that does not diminish God at all. It does not stop Him from being God. It is just that when God entered into covenant with us, He put boundaries around Himself. He has entered into covenant relationship with His people, and that covenant has parameters. It has clear guidelines and clear standards by which He operates.

God saw the wickedness of Sodom and came down to destroy the city because, like Babylon, its sins had reached Heaven. He had heard the cry of its wickedness and its evil, and He had come down to destroy it. And as He came down to destroy the city, He stopped off at Abraham's tent, He fellowshipped with Abraham, and He told him what He was going to do. Abraham, in Scripture, is spoken of as a prophet of God. As God's prophetic people, we should know what God wants to do. That is what being prophetic people means, to know what God is doing. So God stopped off at Abraham's tent to let Him know what He was doing. He said, "*Shall I hide from Abraham what I am about to do?*" (Gen. 18:17). God does not want to hide His purposes from us. God is going to destroy Babylon. We need to hear that loud and clear. Abraham heard that Sodom was about to be destroyed.

And Abraham began his plea to God: "Surely you will not do that if there are twenty righteous people."

"No, if there are twenty I will spare it."

"What about ten?"

"If there are ten I will spare it."

Of course the sad thing was that there was not even that many. There was only one righteous man in the whole of the city, and God had determined to bring the city to destruction, but He would not do it while Lot was there. God knows how to deliver the righteous, and God sent an angel to bring Lot out of Sodom, and as soon as he was away, the fire of destruction fell and the judgment of God came (see 2 Pet. 2:7).

Now Babylon is a worse scenario. It is worse than Sodom because Sodom was never the bride of Christ. Sodom was never the people of the Lord, but Jerusalem was. Jerusalem has become Babylon, and its destruction is therefore inevitable. But before He destroys it, God still rescues His people. In fact, church history tells us of believers in Jerusalem at this time who, because of a prophetic word, fled the city before the destruction came. And so God's call, "Come out from her, My people," which was first heard back in the Old Testament when God was calling His people back out of Babylon into the land of their inheritance, is heard again. God continues to call, and He calls again and again until all His people are safe, until all His children are home, until everyone has escaped from the horrors, the drunkenness, the wantonness, the adultery, and the evil that is rampant in Babylon.

The Two Cities

As we have seen, the Bible is a story of two cities. If Charles Dickens had not taken it already, we could have called the Bible "The Tale of Two Cities." It is the story of two women, two sons, and two mountains. It is the story of conflict between those contrasting characteristics. There is war between Zion and Babylon. There is war between Isaac and Ishmael.

There is war between Sarah and Hagar. There is war between the prostitute and the bride. You are either one or the other. There is no middle ground. There is no neutral land in which both sides can feel secure. You cannot belong to both. Paul says you cannot drink the cup of the Lord and the cup of demons, and Babylon is described as this wanton harlot with a cup full of adulteries and abominations that she holds out for the world to drink and get drunk on. Listen to what happens to Babylon:

> *They will throw dust on their heads, and with weeping and mourning cry out: "Woe! Woe, O great city, where all who had ships on the sea became rich through her wealth! In one hour she has been brought to ruin! Rejoice over her, O Heaven! Rejoice, saints and apostles and prophets! God has judged her for the way she treated you." Then a mighty angel picked up a boulder the size of a large millstone and threw it into the sea, and said: "With such violence the great city of Babylon will be thrown down, never to be found again. The music of harpists and musicians, flute players and trumpeters, will never be heard in you again. No workman of any trade will ever be found in you again. The sound of a millstone will never be heard in you again. The light of a lamp will never shine in you again. The voice of bridegroom and bride will never be heard in you again. Your merchants were the world's great men. By your magic spell all the nations were led astray. In her was found the blood of prophets and of the saints, and of all who have been killed on the earth"* (Revelation 18:19-24).

Her whole society, whether it is her commerce, her arts, or just the activities of everyday family life, have all come to ruin and the reason is that she is the one who was drunk on the blood of the saints. She was the one whose insatiable appetite and blood lust drove her to kill the people of God, and the blood of all the saints and the prophets was found in her. Back in Matthew's Gospel we find Jesus saying to the Jewish leaders, "*Fill up, then, the measure of the sin of your forefathers!*" (Matt. 23:32), just as the sin of Babylon was filled up. He then continues,

> *You snakes! You brood of vipers! How will you escape being condemned to hell? Therefore I am sending you prophets and wise men and teachers. Some of them you will kill and crucify; others you will flog in your synagogues and pursue from town to town. And so upon you will come all the righteous blood that has been shed on earth, from the blood of righteous Abel to the blood of Zechariah son of Berekiah, whom you murdered between the temple and the altar. I tell you the truth, all this will come upon this generation* (Matthew 23:33-36).

We cannot escape the fact that it was this generation that was visited by the judgments of God, that it was this generation, these inhabitants of Jerusalem, that were visited with God's judgment. For God will remove all that defiles, all that breaks covenant, all that rebels.

The Entrance of the Bride

The fall of Babylon means the emergence of Zion. The fall of the prostitute leaves the way open for the bride to come forth. Just as Babylon's hill crumbles and Zion's mountain emerges, just as the prostitute collapses and the bride comes forth, both those things will happen together. We have seen this strange enigma, and yet this continual spiritual truth that the same event means death to some but life to others, condemnation for some but salvation to others. Here God is enacting His judgments, and not because He is a vindictive God. Rather, He is a God of justice, and justice demands that judgments be made. But He removes the prostitute because He has something better. He removes Babylon because He has something of greater beauty. He has a bride to bring forth. He has a bride to show to the world. Babylon is cast into the sea like a great millstone. Jerusalem is cast into the sea like a great mountain. For those who offend God's little ones, it would be better that a millstone be tied around their necks and they be cast into the sea. Egypt went down into the depths of the Red Sea, the prophet tells us, like a stone. Everything that offends will go back to the abyss. Everything that offends will be dropped into the deep. Everything that withstands God will be plunged into the depths of the rebellious ocean, kept there until the final Day of Judgment when all will stand before His throne. The Book of Revelation says there is coming a time when the sea will give up its dead.

> *After this I heard what sounded like the roar of a great multitude in Heaven shouting: "Hallelujah! Salvation and glory and power belong to our God, for true and just are His judgments"* (Revelation 19:1-2).

When Abraham stood before God and was told of the judgment that was going to come upon Sodom, he found solace and confidence in this conviction: surely the judge of all the earth will do right (see Gen. 18:25).

> *After this I heard what sounded like the roar of a great multitude in heaven shouting: "Hallelujah! Salvation and glory and power belong to our God, For true and just are His judgments. He has condemned the great prostitute who corrupted the earth by her adulteries. He has avenged on her the blood of His servants." And again they shouted: "Hallelujah! The smoke from her goes up for ever and ever." The twenty-four elders and the four living creatures fell down and worshiped God, who was seated on the throne. And they cried: "Amen, Hallelujah!" Then a voice came from the throne, saying: "Praise our God, all you His servants, you who fear Him, both small and great!" Then I heard what sounded like a great multitude, like the roar of rushing waters and like loud peals of thunder, shouting: "Hallelujah! For our Lord God Almighty reigns. Let us rejoice and be glad and give Him glory! For the wedding of the Lamb has come, and His bride has made herself ready"* (Revelation 19:1-7).

You see, these two great events are intimately related. As God pulls down Babylon, He builds up Zion. As Babylon devours herself, the bride makes herself ready. There is a time coming, and already is, when everything that defiles is removed, everything that corrupts will be vanquished, everything that dares to take its stand against Christ and dares to revel in its own lordship will be overcome so that only the Kingdom, the King and his bride, the Church, will be seen. What a great day! What a glorious day! What a day to anticipate! What a day to dream of! And when it arrives we will discover that the reality is greater even than the dream.

CHAPTER 10
Enter the Bride

The Bible is a single work; it is not a collection of disjointed books. Across the Scriptures we find common themes and patterns. They move in and out of the books of the Bible like threads on the back of a great tapestry. In looking only at the back of the tapestry you do not see the glorious picture that is being woven, but when you turn the tapestry around and look at the front, you see the picture as it was intended. The themes that weave themselves in and out of the books of the Bible have come together to form a great panorama of the purposes of God from beginning to end.

The Prostitute and the Wife of Noble Character

The major themes of the Bible can sometimes be discovered in surprising places. The Book of Proverbs, for example, is a collection of sayings full of moral warnings with advice to young men and old to avoid the adulteress, to stay away from the prostitute, and to be careful of the unfaithful wife (see for example Prov. 2:16-19; 5:3-20; 6:23-26; 7:1-27; 9:15-18; 23:27-28; 29:3; 30:20; 31:3). These are severe warnings. But they are not just moral lessons; they are also spiritual lessons. There is a temptress who would lure us away from the things of God. These Scriptures unveil a hidden evil. They issue us with a warning that we should consider seriously.

Thankfully, the Book of Proverbs ends on a happier note. There is a wife of noble character (see Prov. 31:10-12, 29-31). The climax of the book is an ideal of faithfulness and family life, of a wife who brings nothing but honor to her husband, a wife in whom he can delight. This could be the story of Christ and the Church. Jesus is seeking a wife of noble character, a wife who is more valuable than rubies. He has eschewed the prostitute and cast out the adulteress. He has set His love upon the one who has captured His heart.

God Loves a Wedding

Jesus began His ministry at a wedding, where He demonstrated the power of the coming Kingdom by turning water into wine. Finally when history comes to its climax and the purposes of God are forever finished, it will be at a wedding: "*For the wedding of the Lamb has come, and His bride has made herself ready*" (Rev. 19:7). In the beginning, when God creates all things, He adds an epilogue to every day of creation by saying, "It is good." This goes on until one day He says, "It is not good." This is not that something has gone wrong; God has not made a mistake. He says, "*It is not good for the man to be alone*" (Gen. 2:18), and what unfolds next is a divine comedy.

God is a God who loves humor. We are made in the image of God, and like God we love to laugh. God says, "I need a bride for my son, Adam," so He brings the animals to Adam as if it were a beauty contest. The animals parade before Adam, and he identifies, gives a name to, each of them. In naming the animals Adam acts prophetically, because he is interpreting the work of God and helping the creatures understand who they are. But Adam does not find a suitable companion from among the animals. There is no creature that corresponds to him. Can you see the humor? Adam needs a wife—an elephant walks by. He is overawed by the power and majesty of a God who can create such a thing, but he does not feel a stirring in the depth of his soul. God knows what He is doing. Adam was never supposed to fall in love with an animal. What God is showing us is something profound and highlighted in the Book of Revelation—we are not supposed to relate to the beast.

At the point when it becomes clear that there is no animal to correspond to Adam, God moves from comedy to intense drama. God puts Adam into a deep sleep. He opens up Adam's side, takes a rib and fashions it into a woman. He does not take a bone from Adam's head that she might dominate him, and He does not take a bone from his foot that he might trample her. He takes it from his side that she might stand beside him, equal to him. He takes it from under his arm that he might protect her. He takes it from near his heart, that he might love her (see Matthew Henry's Commentary). When Adam wakes, God presents the woman to him. Moses' commentary on this is, "*For this reason a man will leave his father and mother and be united to his wife, and they will become one flesh*" (Gen. 2:24). In his letter to the Ephesians, Paul quotes these words and interprets them to refer to the mystical relationship between Jesus and his Church (see Eph. 5:31-33).

Like Adam, Jesus went into a deep sleep, but far deeper than the one Adam experienced. He went into the sleep of death. As He hung dead on the cross, they opened up His side, and out of His side came blood and water (see John 19:34), the very elements that God would use to make a bride for His Son: blood to redeem her and water to wash and prepare her for the day of her wedding (see Heb. 9:19,22).

The Hero Gets the Girl

It is not just in myths, legends, and fairytales that the hero gets the bride. In the Bible you will discover the genesis of that idea. It's a biblical truth. When Joseph interpreted Pharaoh's dream, he was made second in command in Egypt. His wisdom and ability to strategize saved Egypt from starvation. Furthermore, the whole world went down to Egypt to buy corn. Joseph saved a nation from disaster and launched a heroic rescue operation throughout the wider world. Raised up by God to feed men, he was rewarded with the hand of a beautiful bride.

When Caleb, one of only two survivors of the wilderness wanderings, came into the land of promise, he stood in the foothills of the mountains where he had walked 40 years before. He removed his sandals and ran his toes through the grass, smelled the familiar scents of the countryside, and all the old expectations and hopes sprang up in his heart again, and he declared: "I may be old but I still have strength and vitality.

I am still strong in God to go out in battle and come back again." However, he knew that his role was to help shape the next generation, so he decided "*I will give my daughter Acsah in marriage to the man who attacks and captures Kiriath Sepher*" (Josh. 15:16). That tells us something about Acsah. She must have been extremely beautiful, because no man would risk his life for a hag!

In response, Caleb's nephew Othniel went out to take the city. Scripture tells us two important facts about this city. First, we read that giants lived there. Second, its name was Debir, which means, "Word." But previously the city had been called Kiriath Sepher, which means, "City of Books." This city was a seat of learning and knowledge. It was a university town. This town was home to the philosophies of the Canaanite enemy; to take the land they must first bring down the town's philosophies. The struggle was not just against the physical mass of a giant. Before we can take our world we have to bring down its philosophies.

Samson and David were both heroes who won beautiful brides. On the way to meet the girl he wished to marry, Samson encountered a lion, and the Spirit of the Lord came upon him in power so that he tore the lion apart with his bare hands. Later, when Samson found the carcass of the lion swarming with bees, he composed a riddle, "*Out of the eater, something to eat; out of the strong, something sweet*" (Judg. 14:14), to describe how he "the strong" wins "the sweet"—the bride.

David won his bride by defeating the Philistines. He arrived on the battlefield as the armies of the Lord were being threatened and ridiculed by the Philistines, whose champion,

Goliath, was a nine-foot giant. He learned that Saul had promised a reward to whoever killed the Philistine champion—an exemption from taxes and the hand of his daughter Mirab in marriage. This is the champion's reward.

In Scripture the champion is not an athlete or the winner of the egg-and-spoon race. He is an outstanding warrior. In Psalm 45 there is a picture of a heavenly bridegroom subduing all his enemies while celebrating the love of a beautifully prepared bride. This psalm is full of Messianic concepts and insights.

Compared to all these heroes, Jesus is the ultimate hero. He has come to feed a starving world. He has come to pull down every false philosophy and bring it into obedience to His lordship and His Word. He has come to trample the lion underfoot. He has come to kill the giant. He deserves the bride. God loves weddings, and He has arranged a wedding for his Son. God wants to see the wedding of His Son just as Abraham wanted to see the wedding of Isaac, but he did not want his son to take a wife from among the Canaanites. Abraham called his trusted servant, who had stewardship of all he owned, and he loaded him with gifts and sent him on a journey to find a bride for Isaac. He sent him back to his own people, and there the servant saw a woman watering her camels. When he was sure that she was the right woman, he showed her his master's treasure and persuaded her to return with him to marry his master's son.

In the same way, the Father in Heaven has sent forth the steward of His house with a message for us, "Will you come back and marry my master's son?' He has come to His Church, and He has shown us His gifts, His grace, and His anointing, and, overwhelmed by His generosity, we have said, "Yes! We will come." We have not seen Him yet, but we are persuaded. The description He has brought us and the story so far is enough.

In Scripture wars and weddings are not incompatible concepts. We have already seen how Othniel returned from a battle to claim his bride. Samson defeated a lion to get his bride. David killed a giant and won his bride. In the nineteenth chapter of Revelation, war and wedding go hand in hand. There is a rider on a white horse dressed in fine linen, and He leads the armies of Heaven out to battle—and the bride has gone to war in her wedding dress! The "*fine linen, bright and clean*" of her wedding dress is the "*fine linen, white and clean*" of her warfare. She is following the bridegroom and sharing in His victory.

The Bride Makes Herself Ready

Remember that the Book of Revelation is a series of action replays. In chapter 19 we have a description of the bride who has made herself ready. In chapter 21 we have a much fuller description in terms of the holy city:

> *Then I saw a new Heaven and a new earth, for the first Heaven and the first earth had passed away, and there was no longer any sea. I saw the Holy City, the new Jerusalem, coming down out of Heaven from God, prepared as a bride beautifully dressed for her husband* (Revelation 21:1-2).

This is the holy city of which we are citizens. This is the church of which we are members. As you look out on the church in the world and see it divided and defiled, it is difficult to imagine that this is its destiny. Yet the evidence of its triumph is more real than what we see before our eyes. For who could believe even for a moment that Jesus, who shed His blood to possess a beautiful bride, would be satisfied with the decrepit and ugly church we can so often see in the world. He came to redeem her with His blood and wash her with the water of the Word, and this Word will penetrate the hearts and minds of the redeemed. The Bible will no longer be a book of mystery gathering dust on a shelf, never read, never put into action. There is a time coming when the Word of God will be unbound. There is a time coming when things will change because God will say, "So far and no farther!" There are days of preparation at hand. God will not allow His bride to walk this world in filthy clothes. His promise in Old Testament Scriptures stands:

> *He has clothed me with garments of salvation and arrayed me in a robe of righteousness, as a bridegroom adorns his head like a priest, and as a bride adorns herself with her jewels* (Isaiah 61:10).

The Church comes forth full of gifts and graces. Most importantly she is coming down from Heaven. She comes down from above. Her life source is in Heaven.

That does not mean she is going to suddenly arrive on the doorstep like Mary Poppins. When it says she comes down out of Heaven, it is telling us that all the life and gifting of the church comes from God. As James writes, "*Every good and perfect gift is from above, coming down from the Father*" (James 1:17). The life-source of the church is God himself. The church is different from everything else. She has a beauty that surpasses that of the prostitute who, with all the cosmetic surgery and makeup in the world, could not ever begin to imitate her. The prostitute sparkles, but the bride shines. The world is full of imitations that sparkle, but there is only one bride, and she shines with the beauty of God.

The bride is to show the world the glory of the bridegroom. The bride also wants to make herself ready for her husband. This is an amazing thing. In His mercy and grace God allows us to work with Him. We believe in the sovereignty of God. We believe that before the foundation of the world we were chosen in Christ according to His purpose. But there are actions we can take to cooperate with God in bringing His purpose to pass.

This does not mean that God needs us. There are those who believe that they are there to get God out of a hole. The truth is that God has done very well without us, and when we are dead and gone, He will continue to do well. The Bible tells us that "*the grace of God that brings salvation has appeared to all men. It teaches us to say 'No' to ungodliness and worldly passions, and to live self-controlled, upright and godly lives in this present age*" (Titus 2:11-12). We can resist the devil, and he will flee from us. We can overcome temptation. What is more, we can do things for ourselves that we once thought only God could do. Many people ask for prayer for things that God has said they should do for themselves. One says, "I am plagued by the old nature. Could you pray that I get rid of my old nature?" God says, "*Put off your old self*" (Eph. 4:22). Another says, "I want to be holy." God says, "*Be holy, because I am holy*" (1 Pet. 1:16); we can be holy because "*everything we need for life and godliness*" (2 Pet. 1:3) has already been given to us in Christ.

But this does not mean that we are left entirely to our own devices. I am not a do-it-yourself expert. If I begin a job in my home, experience tells me that somewhere along the line I am going to have to call an expert in. Then not only does he have to finish the job, he has to undo the work that I began. Help is at hand. In the same way, every ministry under whose influence we sit is there to equip us. This is how Paul spoke to the Corinthians: "*I promised you to one husband, to Christ, so that I might present you as a pure virgin to Him*" (2 Cor. 11:2). Those of us who have responsibility in the church are there to help the bride get ready. People must help themselves, but there are areas of expertise where they can call in help. There are areas of revelation that individuals will never achieve on their own. That is why we need one another. There is no such thing as just Jesus and me. The church blesses and edifies herself so she can grow and mature. The ministries that God sends are to help the church prepare herself.

Not only that, but the Lord, the heavenly bridegroom Himself, is involved in the preparations, as Paul writes to the Ephesians:

> *Husbands, love your wives, just as Christ loved the church and gave himself up for her to make her holy, cleansing her by the washing with water through the word, and to present her to himself as a radiant church, without stain or wrinkle or any other blemish, but holy and blameless. In this same way, husbands ought to love their wives as their own bodies. He who loves his wife loves himself. After all, no one ever hated his own body, but he feeds and cares for it, just as Christ does the church—for we are members of his body* (Ephesians 5:25-30).

Paul says, "I want to present you to Christ." Christ says, "I want to present you to myself." We must say, "I want to present myself to Jesus" (see 2 Tim. 2:15).

The Ultimate Wedding

In the opening chapters of Revelation Jesus writes to the churches. He says that they are like those who wear defiled robes and that they need to cover their nakedness. He writes to them because they are not what they should be, and he says: "*He who has an ear, let him hear what the Spirit says to the churches*" (Rev. 2:7). God has a word for the churches, and it is a word that says change, adjust, and overcome.

This is how the Spirit speaks to the churches at the beginning of the Book of Revelation. By the end of the book, the Spirit and the church speak in unison, and so we read of one voice: "*The Spirit and the bride say, 'Come!'*" (Rev. 22:17).

The change that has occurred is the same change that occurs to you in the personal realm. When we came to Jesus, God gave us the Holy Spirit. The Holy Spirit is a vocal Spirit; He continually speaks. He is the Spirit of prophecy, and He cannot keep quiet. When God sent the Spirit into your heart, He came shouting; the Spirit shouted God's love for you. In Galatians we read,

> *But when the time had fully come, God sent His Son, born of a woman, born under law, to redeem those under law, that we might receive the full rights of sons. Because you are sons, God sent the Spirit of His Son into our hearts, the Spirit who calls out, "Abba, Father"* (Galatians 4:4-6).

The Spirit came shouting, "Abba Father," "Daddy God." The Spirit is doing all the shouting because He wants to convince you of the truth of what He is saying. But when we turn to Romans (a book written after Galatians, despite coming first in our Bibles), it says:

> *For you did not receive a spirit that makes you a slave again to fear, but you received the Spirit of sonship. And by Him we cry, "Abba, Father"* (Romans 8:15).

When the Spirit came, He did all the shouting, but when He has convinced us, we shout, too—and we shout exactly the same thing as the Spirit was shouting. Now we find the bride persuaded by the Spirit. We find the bride prepared, so the great shout goes up; the Spirit and the bride say, "Come! Come to the waters, come to the feast, come to the wedding, come to the Lord!"

CHAPTER 11

The Return of the Rider

I saw Heaven standing open and there before me was a white horse, whose rider is called Faithful and True. With justice He judges and makes war. His eyes are like blazing fire, and on His head are many crowns. He has a name written on Him that no one knows but He himself. He is dressed in a robe dipped in blood, and His name is the Word of God. The armies of Heaven were following Him, riding on white horses and dressed in fine linen, white and clean. Out of His mouth comes a sharp sword with which to strike down the nations. "He will rule them with an iron scepter." He treads the winepress of the fury of the wrath of God Almighty. On His robe and on His thigh He has this name written:

KING OF KINGS AND LORD OF LORDS.

—Revelation 19:11-16

There are no prizes for guessing who is being described here. The name Jesus does not appear, but there is an abundance of evidence to indicate that this is none other than the Lamb of God, the Lord Jesus Christ Himself. We saw Him riding out victoriously at the beginning of the book, and since the moment He rolled the scroll out (see Revelation 5), He has been busy riding through the earth bent on conquest. He has been bringing lives in submission to His lordship. He has been turning nations to the ways of the truth. As He rides forth now in all His splendor, He is crowned with many crowns because He is the King of Kings. Other kings have surrendered their crowns to the Christ. Just as the elders, who adore Him, cast their crowns before Him, the rulers of this world—the principalities and powers that govern our society—must fall at His feet and cast their crowns before Him. And He takes each crown and sets it upon His own head.

He is taking up the crowns of the nations because God had made an offer that He could not refuse. God had said, "*Ask of Me, and I will make the nations Your inheritance, the ends of the earth Your possession. You will rule them with an iron scepter*" (Ps. 2:8-9). Can you imagine that Jesus would refuse such an offer? He has borne the sin of the world, taken upon Himself the curse of creation, obliterated sin through His death on the cross, made propitiation for all men everywhere, and accomplished all the work God gave Him to do. He endured the cross for the joy that was set before Him. This joy was like the joy of the harvest, for there would come a great ingathering, and nations would bow to His lordship.

We have not yet seen this in its fullness. There have been fleeting moments in history. There have been seasons of revival where whole nations seem to have been moved and swayed by the wind of the Spirit, but there is coming a day when whole nations, policy makers, politicians, and social engineers, everyone of influence in the nations of the world, will be bowing to his lordship. The process has begun, and it has been in operation for over 2,000 years. It will come to a glorious climax, for the end will come when this Gospel of the kingdom has been preached as a testimony to all nations (see Matt. 24:14). Jesus sent out His followers and said, "*Make disciples of all nations*" (Matt. 18:19). When Jesus comes again and judges the world, He will separate the sheep from the goats. The sheep and the goats are not individuals; they are nations. There is a time coming when nations will turn to Christ. This does not necessarily mean that every citizen of that nation will be born again, but it does mean that a critical mass of believers will have such influence, such authority, and such power that others, if they know what is good for them, will listen to and heed their voice. This will not be a time for the church to flex its muscles and show how clever it is, but it will come about because "*Righteousness exalts a nation, but sin is a disgrace to any people*" (Prov. 14:34).

The King and His Army

I sometimes like to go into art galleries. I like art that is dramatic. You may go into a gallery and see one of those huge paintings, almost like a mural, so many feet long, high, and wide, a great panoramic view. I like to look at those that depict battle scenes. The drama is all there: the smoke, the flashes of the cannon in the distance, the horses clearly ready to advance, and all the weapons drawn. You see the great chief, the leader of the army. You recognize him not just by his noble stance but by the size and the stature of the horse that he is sitting on; and you look and think, "What a hero! What a fine figure! What an inspiring leader!" You get close and look at the detail, but then you step back to see the panorama of the view, and as you step back, you see that although he is the focus of attention, although he occupies center stage, and although he is the one around whom everything else revolves, there are others in this picture. As you step back, you see that he is a leader, but he has an army. They, too, are poised to move forward; they have weapons drawn, and they also have the glint of warfare in their eye.

The rider on the white horse does not go alone; a multitude goes with him. As you look closer at those who are arrayed in his train, awaiting his command, you begin to recognize them, too. You look at the leader, and you say to yourself, "I know Him! It's Jesus." But this is not just a portrait of Jesus; it is also a portrait of us, the church. We are included in His triumph. He has a heavenly army that obeys His will and an earthly army that follows the Lamb wherever He goes. The armies of Heaven are following Him. It is *armies*—in plural—because the Lord has two armies. Our fight is not against flesh and blood. The earth is the battleground of our Gospel enterprise, but we wrestle against principalities and powers in the heavenly places. We need to constantly remind ourselves of this, though some believers in our generation seem to be obsessed with it. When we ride out, the angelic army accompanies us. There may be demons in the world, but there are angels with the church. There is an unseen host sent forth by Jesus to minister to those who are the heirs of salvation. He will give His angels charge over you in case you strike your foot on a stone.

When Elisha was in Dothan, an enemy king wanted to capture him because he had been giving away the king's secret strategy. What the king plotted in secret Elisha heard in the Spirit, and so the king decided that if he was going to win the war, he needed to get rid of the prophet. He sent a whole army to capture this one man. Early in the morning, the servant of Elisha went out to the front door, and he caught a glimpse of a strange and unusual glint in the hills and the mountains that surrounded the prophet's house. As he looked more closely, he saw that it was nothing less than the early morning sun reflecting on spears and shields of a vast army that had come to capture the prophet of God. He ran back inside to tell the prophet that they were in trouble, but the old man simply made a request of God. He asked the Lord to open the young man's eyes. Of course, the young man's eyes could not have been more open. They were out like organ stops! He was like a character from a cartoon. It was not the eyes of his head that needed enlightening, but rather the eyes of his heart. God opened his eyes, and the servant saw that all around the prophet were the fiery chariots of God. Of course, Elisha knew they were there all the time. The old man had said to his servant, "*Those who are with us are more than those who are with them*" (2 Kings 6:16).

That is still true today. There may be demons, there may be principalities and powers, and there may be hideous hordes let loose in our world bent on corrupting our society. But here is the good news: there are more with us than there are with them! "*The chariots of God are tens of thousands and thousands of thousands,*" David declared (Ps. 68:17). We do not need to work out the number with a calculator. What he is telling us is that they are innumerable! The numbers of the angels that we saw surrounding the throne and worshiping the Lamb are myriads and myriads, and these angels are with us. God has sent them to minister to us, to camp around us, to watch over us, and to be part of the great advancing and unstoppable army of Heaven that is determined to fill the earth with the glory of God.

The Name that Nobody Knows

I like the mystery that there is a name written on Jesus that nobody knows but He Himself. As soon as I read that, I wanted to know what the name is. My wife used to tell me that I am nosy. I used to tell her that I am just interested. There are certain things that make my fingers itch. Letters that come through the door addressed to somebody else that say "Private and Confidential," or doors that say "Strictly No Admittance." So as Jesus rides forth with this unknown name and the great armies of Heaven following behind Him, if you hear a thunder of hooves moving faster than the rest, the flash of a rider going past you making his way to the front of the column, it is only me trying to read the name that nobody knows but Jesus Himself!

I like the fact that He has got a name on Him that nobody knows. I still want to find out what it is, but I thank God for the mystery that there still remains about the Son. Paul prayed for the Ephesians that God would open the eyes of their hearts so that they might know Him better. We speak about coming to know Jesus, but that is just our first encounter. There is an eternity of relationship with Him, and eternity will not be long enough to fathom all the mysteries of Christ, because in Him "*are hidden all the treasures of wisdom and knowledge*" (Col. 2:3). Some people say, "What are you going to do in eternity? How are you going to fill up all that time?" I will tell you: finding out more about Jesus, discovering new facets of the Lamb, walking in the paths of the good shepherd, beholding His radiant glory! I will follow Him, and I will follow Him as closely as I can because I am trying to read the name on Him that nobody knows but He Himself.

You can get books that explain the hard sayings of the Bible, but I like the lingering mystery. I like the spiritual uncertainties that remain in the Word of God. I do not think we are supposed to understand it all logically. The writer to the Hebrews said, "*By faith we understand that the universe was formed at God's command*" (Heb. 11:3). There are some things we understand even though we do not know them. One day Elijah the prophet came to Elisha. He threw his cloak around him, and Elisha was changed forever. All Elisha asked was to go home and kiss his mother and father good-bye, and then he would follow the prophet. Elijah said to him, "You do what you like. What have I done to you?" Elisha did not know, nor could he explain what had happened to him deep on the inside. He could not put it into words. He could only say "I just know that I was touched, and I will never be the same again." There are communications in the Spirit that defy our understanding.

Paul said that he communicated with spiritual people in spiritual ways:

> *This is what we speak, not in words taught us by human wisdom but in words taught by the Spirit, expressing spiritual truths in spiritual words* (1 Corinthians 2:13).

One version speaks of "speaking spirituals to the spiritual." There is a communication that goes on in the Spirit that has nothing to do with logic. There is a communication that goes on in the Spirit that has nothing to do with intellect. It is deep calling unto deep.

I could not stand up with Professor Hawkins and have a physics debate and prove to him by my superior knowledge how the world came into being. I simply understand by faith that the worlds were made by the Word of God. I have a spiritual understanding. I am not suggesting that as believers we need to kiss our brains good-bye. God gave you ability and an intellect, and you should pursue it to the ultimate. But when you and I speak in tongues, when we pray to God in the Spirit, our mind is unfruitful, though in the Spirit we are speaking mysteries. That is why you can receive a revelation that is totally new to you and yet somehow it is strangely familiar. It is like an old friend you have never met before, but you have been spiritually prepared and so welcome him without fear.

We know Jesus but still we want to know Him. Consider how Paul puts it in Philippians. He is categorizing and cataloging all the things that were assumed to be beneficial for him in his chosen career in religion: a Hebrew of the Hebrews, circumcised on the eighth day, a Pharisee, guiltless as far as the Law is concerned, persecuting the church in his zeal—and then he says this:

> *But whatever was to my profit I now consider loss for the sake of Christ. What is more, I consider everything a loss compared to the surpassing greatness of knowing Christ Jesus my Lord, for whose sake I have lost all things. I consider them rubbish, that I may gain Christ and be found in Him, not having a righteousness of my*

> *own that comes from the law, but that which is through faith in Christ—the righteousness that comes from God and is by faith. I want to know Christ and the power of His resurrection and the fellowship of sharing in His sufferings, becoming like Him in His death, and so, somehow, to attain to the resurrection from the dead* (Philippians 3:7-11).

The actual language here is very colorful, and Eugene Peterson brings it out in *The Message*, when he has Paul comparing everything that was gain to him as if it were dog dung. That is actually a good rendition of what Paul is saying here. "*When I consider everything that was to my account,*" he says, "*it is like so much dog dung compared to knowing Christ Jesus my Lord*" (Phil. 3:8 TM).

I guess you would have to know Jesus pretty well to be able to consider everything that the world thought was worthy as dog dung. You would need to have more than a nodding acquaintance with Jesus. He must have known Jesus intimately. But then he says, "I want to know Him!" You know what he means. Those of us who know Christ have one burning passion—we want to know Him. Jesus said, "If you eat the bread I give you, you will never hunger. If you drink the water I give you, you will never thirst" (see John 4:14; 6:35). That is true, but He did not tell us that we were going to get addicted to the bread and the water. You thought if you took just one sip and one nibble then that would be enough for life; but it created a greater desire, a deeper longing, and now you find yourself wanting to drink at the living fountainhead and eat the bread of life. You have an appetite for it although you are not hungry. You have a desire for it although you are not thirsty.

Three Other Names

The strange thing about this short passage is that although it tells us that He has a name written on Him that nobody knows but He Himself, it also gives Him three other names. This just deepens the enigma. He has got a name that we do not know, but He is called...—and then we are given three names. John tells us this: "*I saw Heaven standing open and there before me was a white horse, whose rider is called Faithful and True*" (Rev. 19:11).

Faithful and True

The one who leads us is faithful and true. Faithfulness is one of the watchwords of the Book of Revelation. It is an awesome quality. It is not faith, nor is it being full of faith. Faithfulness means loyalty. And it seems to me that God puts as much store in faithfulness as He does in faith. God is looking for those who are faithful and true. You see, the one we follow determines what we will be like. If we follow one whose name is Faithful and True, it is because God wants us to become faithful and true. We are looking for men of faith, but God is looking for faithful men and faithful women. The Bible asks, "*A faithful man who can find*" (Prov. 20:6). There are many who seek their own way, but God is looking for a people who are faithful unto death, a people who will not choose their own path, who will not determine their own future, who will not follow their own imagined destiny, but who will follow the Lamb faithfully. Jesus tells us Himself that He did nothing when He was here on earth except what He saw the Father doing. He spoke no word but the words that the Father gave Him to speak. How can we be sure that our faith is the right faith? Our faith is centered in the faithful one. He was not a confidence trickster or a madman. He was not a religious fanatic. He was not someone who had been tipped over the edge in His own imaginings. He was not the crusader of a new cult. He was the Son of God who had come into the world to lead us faithfully into all truth. It is the very essence of His character. He is faithful and true.

The Word of God

As we continue reading we find that his name is also "the Word of God." This is one of the clues that connect the Book of Revelation to the Gospel of John, because this is one of John's great descriptions of Christ. When he described Jesus coming into the world in his Gospel, he began by telling us, "*In the beginning was the Word, and the Word was with God, and the Word was God. He was with God in the beginning. Through Him all things were made; without Him nothing was made that has been made*" (John 1:1-3). He is the great creative Word who came to reveal the Father to us: "*The Word became flesh and made His dwelling among us. We have seen His glory, the glory of the One and Only, who came from the Father, full of grace and truth*" (John 1:14). Jesus has come down as God's ultimate word. The writer to the Hebrews says,

> *In the past God spoke to our forefathers through the prophets at many times and in various ways, but in these last days He has spoken to us by His Son, whom He appointed heir of all things, and through whom He made the universe* (Hebrews 1:1-2).

He is God's last word, and God's last word will last for millennia. It is not God's last word, and then there is no other word. Jesus is the eternal last word of God. There is nothing to add after Jesus has spoken. There is no more revelation to come after Jesus has shone upon us. Everything that you and I can know about the Father is in the Son. Paul describes it like this: "*In Christ all the fullness of the Deity lives in bodily form*" (Col. 2:9). When Jesus came into the world He was the Son. We do not believe in three gods. We believe in a Trinitarian godhead. But everything you could know was in the Son. One of His disciples asked Him one day to show him the Father. Jesus replied, "*Anyone who has seen Me has seen the Father. How can you say, 'Show us the Father'?*" (John 14:8-9).

If you want to know the Father, all you have to do is look at the Son. If you want to know the Spirit, look at the Son, because the fullness of the Godhead dwells in him. He is God in the flesh. He is God's last word, His great explanation. He came in bodily form because natural men cannot receive the things of the Spirit. I suppose Jesus could have come down here like the Holy Spirit, powerful but unseen. He could have come like some great divine influence among the nations, turning hearts, touching lives, and healing bodies. But that would have been like the wind. You can see what it does, but you do not know where it comes from, and you do not know where it is going.

To know God, to relate to Him, we have to see something, and so the Word became flesh and dwelled among us. He took on bodily form. Now interestingly, the only place in Scripture other than Colossians where the expression "bodily form" is used comes in the Gospels where God tells John the Baptist that the one who is coming is the Messiah, and John asks how he will recognize Him. He is told "*The man on whom you see the Spirit come down and remain is He*" (John 1:33). But how do you see the Spirit? You can see the effects of the Spirit, but you cannot see the Spirit. So when Jesus came up out of the waters at His baptism, Heaven was opened, and the Spirit descended in bodily form like a dove. Why? Because John had to see Him. Now the world needs to see something, and just as Jesus in His earthly ministry was the fullness of the Godhead, the church must now be the fullness of Christ.

It must demonstrate the life of Jesus in a tangible, audible, and visual way to a world that has no clue about seeing spiritual things. We have to flesh it out. Just as He rides ahead of us as the Word of God made flesh, so we ride behind Him as the army of Heaven, His word made flesh in us so that men might see our good works and glorify our Father who is in Heaven. The natural man cannot receive the things of the Spirit. They are foolishness to him. But you show him a sign and a wonder, you show him a community of faith and love, you show him a people of good works, and they will be cut to the heart and fall down and confess that God is with you.

King of Kings and Lord of Lords

Finally, we are told that Jesus has another name. In fact, it is so important that in my Bible it is in capital letters. It is so important that the Scripture says He has it written on Him twice. If I can say this reverently, it is as if Jesus is riding out in a tracksuit, ready for action. You see people who think they are ready for action. They come out in their tracksuit with "Adidas" across the chest and "Adidas" down the leg. That is Jesus. It is very confusing when people come out with "Adidas" across the chest and "Puma" down the leg. You are not quite sure who they are! But the name that is written on Jesus describes who He is, helps us understand what He is going to do, and gives us confidence in the outcome of it all. He is called "KING OF KINGS AND LORD OF LORDS." He is the king of all those who are ruling and all those who are lording; and every king and every lord shall ultimately bow the knee and confess that Jesus Christ is Lord to the glory of God the Father.

CHAPTER 12
The Millennium

For this chapter you will need to read Revelation 20:1-10. This is the passage of Scripture upon which people's perception of the Book of Revelation rests. Commentators are categorized on their handling of the Book of Revelation by this one issue—are they premillennialist, amillennialist, or postmillennialist? Putting it simply, a premillennialist believes that Jesus will come physically on the earth, probably to a throne in natural Jerusalem, and will reign over our world for a thousand years. Amillennialists believe that the present age is the millennium. There is no special sign or wonder or growth necessary. It is the millennium, and Jesus could come back at any moment and usher in the end of all things. Postmillennialists believe that the church of Christ will increasingly triumph in the world and will bring in the

Kingdom before the King returns. That is, the millennial rule of Christ will be seen and experienced in our earth before Jesus comes again.

Seizing the Dragon

So to understand this passage let us look firstly at the dragon. We see an angel coming down out of Heaven, having the key to the abyss and holding in his hand a great chain; he seizes the dragon and binds him for a thousand years. In Job God describes two great beasts, a beast from the land and a beast from the sea. The beast from the land in chapter 40 is called Behemoth. The beast from the sea in chapter 41 is called Leviathan. Leviathan is the monster of the deep that is recorded and spoken of in Psalms and in the prophet Isaiah. He is also the beast from the sea described in the thirteenth chapter of Revelation. It is an amazing description, and the object of the exercise is that God wants to ask Job if he can overcome this great monster.

You would benefit at this point from reading chapter 41 of the Book of Job. You will see that Leviathan is quite terrifying! And in the light of his awesome appearance and his immeasurable strength, God asks Job these questions: "Can you catch him? Can you tie him up? Can you lead him on a leash? Can you deal with the terrible, awesome power of this beast from the abyss, this monster from the deep?" Of course, the conclusion we are forced to come to is that we are not even going to try! But this is only a picture of an even more fearsome dragon—the ancient serpent, the devil, the devourer, the accuser. He is intimidating to the people of God. There are believers in Christ who live in fear of the devil because they know, as Job knew, that, humanly speaking, they have no hope against such great opposition. But God has bound up the dragon:

> *And I saw an angel coming down out of heaven, having the key to the Abyss and holding in his hand a great chain. He seized the dragon, that ancient serpent, who is the devil, or Satan, and bound him for a thousand years* (Revelation 20:1-2).

The dragon has been caught! The very word seized conveys a kind of violence or at least determination. The angel coming down with the authority of God has all the ability to arrest the dragon in the midst of its evil work. He lays hold of and seizes the dragon. This is the God who seized you, the Christ who laid hold of you. Do you remember how Paul describes his conversion experience, declaring that his one desire was to lay hold of that for which Christ had laid hold of him? The idea behind that word is that he was seized. Christ arrested him. Jesus reached into his life and laid hold of him. When you were a rebel, when you were against Christ, when you went on your way breathing murder, as Paul did on the Damascus Road, Jesus broke into your life and seized you. You and I have been laid hold of by God. And the God who laid hold of us in grace and mercy is the God who has laid hold of the dragon for ultimate destruction.

As we read of the dragon, in Job, God interjects and speaks of His own power and authority, for it far exceeds every other power and authority. Our Lord Jesus has received a name that is above every name: "*All authority in heaven and on earth has been given to me*" (Matt. 28:18). Many believers need still to understand that the struggle in which we are engaged is an unequal struggle and that the battle that is lined up on our planet is between an army that cannot lose and an enemy that cannot win. There is no question about the outcome, for the Lamb has conquered and the dragon has lost. Not only is the dragon caught—an unimaginable thing, for remember that Job stood in amazement to even contemplate that such a beast could be laid hold of—but the dragon's strength dissipates as the powerful hand of the angel of God lays hold of his scales, catches hold of his horns, puts his arm around his neck, and brings him into submission!

Satan Bound

The angel had in his hand a great chain. With it he bound the dragon for a thousand years. Now if we can understand when that happened we can come to terms with when the millennium began. Jesus said this:

> *In fact, no one can enter a strong man's house and carry off his possessions unless he first ties up the strong man. Then he can rob his house* (Mark 3:27).

Jesus utters those words in the context of His miracle ministry. He is casting out demons and says, "*If I drive out demons by the Spirit of God, then the Kingdom of God has come upon you*" (Matt. 12:28). But the reaction of people at that time is to accuse Him of casting out demons by beelzebub, the prince of demons. Jesus explains that that is impossible, because a house divided against itself cannot stand. He then goes into this description of someone coming to the strongman's house and tying up or binding the strongman; Jesus is showing us that when He embarked on His public ministry, when He came preaching the good news and working miracles, when

He started to cast out demons, it was a sign and irrefutable evidence that He had tied up the strongman. Listen to how Luke renders that same Scripture:

> *When a strong man, fully armed, guards his own house, his possessions are safe. But when someone stronger attacks and overpowers him, he takes away the armor in which the man trusted and divides up the spoils* (Luke 11:21-22).

There is no denying that the dragon is strong and powerful. But one stronger than he has come and has tied up the strongman and has bound him with chains for a thousand years.

> *For…God did not spare angels when they sinned, but sent them to hell, putting them into gloomy dungeons* [for some manuscripts, 'into chains of darkness'] *to be held for judgment* (2 Peter 2:4).

Peter is looking back at what God has done in history. Many of the angels who fell did not get free rein to roam about our world. They did not necessarily become the demon powers that affect and influence the lives of people and the affairs of nations. Some of the ringleader angels, angels bent on unspeakable evil, were sent to prison to await the Day of Judgment. They are not loose in our world. He did not send satan to that prison because satan is actually God's satan, and God had some use and purpose for him. But many of the "ringleader" angels were actually sent to hell and to prisons of darkness. Jude puts it even more dramatically:

> *And the angels who did not keep their positions of authority but abandoned their own home—these He has*

> *kept in darkness, bound with everlasting chains for judgment on the great Day* (Jude 6).

It may be, that we will have a part to play in that judgment because Paul tells the Corinthians, *"Do you not know that we will judge angels?"* (1 Cor. 6:3). We do not live in fear of those incarcerated angels. In fact, they live in fearful anticipation of the judgment that we will pass on them. But there are others out there, and what Jesus did when He came into the world was to start to bind up the principalities and powers.

Binding and Loosing

Let me take you to Matthew chapter 16, because not only is Jesus the great Master of destiny and history, He is the one who invites us to work with him in his ministry of overcoming the powers of evil. Here Peter gets a revelation of who Jesus is. I have said it before, but I will emphasize it again, there are too many Christians who are more concerned with finding out who the beast is, there are many Christians who want to know what the number is, and there are many people who want to understand all these deep things of satan—but the key to success and victory is to know who Jesus is!

This revelation comes to Peter:

> *"But what about you?" He asked. "Who do you say I am?" Simon Peter answered, "You are the Christ, the Son of the living God." Jesus replied, "Blessed are you, Simon son of Jonah, for this was not revealed to you by man, but by My Father in heaven. And I tell you that you are Peter, and on this rock I will build My church, and the gates of Hades will not overcome it. I will give*

> *you the keys of the kingdom of heaven; whatever you bind on earth will be bound in heaven, and whatever you loose on earth will be loosed in heaven"* (Matthew 16:15-19).

To those who are built on the foundation of the confession of His lordship, those who constitute his Church, Jesus is saying that He is giving them the keys of the Kingdom so that they can bind and they can loose. It is not that we are the instigators of what we bind and loose; we are the implementers of what God has already bound and loosed, and one of the things that He has already bound is the power of the enemy. If I may speak figuratively, he entrusts the great chain and the key to the abyss, which the angel held, to the Church. In chapter 18 of Matthew's Gospel Jesus speaks on how to correct errors in the church. It is interesting that these are the only two passages in the Gospels where the Church is mentioned. The first one tells us that He is building the Church on a foundation, and the second one is about how the Church is supposed to operate, how we are commanded to forgive one another and called to repent when we are wrong.

> *I tell you the truth, whatever you bind on earth will be bound in heaven, and whatever you loose on earth will be loosed in heaven. Again, I tell you that if two of you on earth agree about anything you ask for, it will be done for you by my Father in heaven. For where two or three come together in my name, there am I with them* (Matthew 18:18-20).

He tells us that this is an activity of the Church. The two witnesses are there to bind and loose because He is with them. Just as He stood in the midst of the lamp stands, He is with His people. Binding and loosing is what Jesus did. Binding and loosing is what we are called to do. The angel took hold of the dragon and bound him with a great chain, and that will not happen in some distant future, but has already happened 2,000 years ago. Through the cross Christ spoiled the principalities and powers and made a show of them openly, triumphing over them through the cross. There is a great hymn that celebrates this:

My heart and voice I raise,
To spread Messiah's praise;
Messiah's praise let all repeat;
The universal Lord,
By whose almighty word
Creation rose in form complete.
A servant's form he wore,
And in his body bore
Our dreadful curse on Calvary:
He like a victim stood,
And poured his sacred blood,
To set the guilty captives free.
But soon the Victor rose
Triumphant o'er his foes,
And led their vanquished host in chains:
He threw their empire down,
His foes compelled to own,
O'er all the great Messiah reigns

Benjamin Rhodes

Satan is bound; but if he was bound 2,000 years ago, does that mean he was released in the year A.D. 1000 because he has only been bound for 1,000 years? If he was only bound for

1,000 years and that was 2,000 years ago, where does that leave us today? It would be worrying unless when John says "one thousand" he does not actually mean a literal thousand. As we have seen, John uses numbers as symbols and not as sums. Sevens speak of completeness. Four has to do with the earth—the four corners of the earth. Twelve has to do with God's Kingdom, His government, and His redeemed people—there are 24 elders and 144,000 who follow the Lamb wherever He goes.

These are numbers that convey completeness and fullness. One thousand is another number that occurs here and elsewhere. There are thousands and thousands and 10,000 times 10,000 angels. This is telling us that the angels are innumerable. The Psalmist tells us that God owns the cattle on a thousand hills. That does not mean that when you get to hill 1,001 they belong to somebody else!

That is what the legalists and the literalists might say. But this is not a legalistic book, and it is not a literalistic book. It is a poetic book. It is a prophetic book. It is a book of sign and symbol, and so when the psalmist speaks of a thousand hills he means every hill everywhere, and when John speaks of 1,000, he is speaking about the whole of the age between Jesus' first coming and His second coming. One thousand is one of those numbers that conveys an ideal, not a calculated number. He is speaking of the age with a progressive expectation of the Kingdom's fulfillment.

When Jesus comes again, He is coming for a pure bride. When Jesus comes again, He is coming for a Kingdom. He is not coming back with a dustpan and brush to pick up the broken pieces of His Church. He is coming back for a Church triumphant that has filled the earth with His glory. Satan is not only caught, he is chained and cast down. The angel took him, bound him, and threw him into the abyss.

There are many clues for us in the Book of Revelation about how the Kingdom operates. You know that the Kingdom has come, is coming, and will come. So we are experiencing the first fruits of the Kingdom, we are experiencing the foretaste, we have tasted of the powers of the age to come, and we are living in that overlap of the "is" and "is to come." We live here on earth, but our citizenship is in Heaven. We are members of his Kingdom even though it has not yet come in all its fullness. So the Book of Revelation also describes for us the fall of satan and the destruction of the evil one in those terms.

In chapter 12, when there was war in Heaven, we saw that satan was hurled out of Heaven down onto the earth. Here in chapter 20 we find that he was thrown down into the abyss, and later on we are going to discover in his final demise that he is thrown into the lake of burning sulfur. So there is a progressive defeat of the evil one. First, he is thrown out of the place of his authority; second, he is bound so that he cannot influence the nations; and ultimately, he is cast into the lake of fire where the beast and the false prophet already are. He will be utterly destroyed, but until he is utterly destroyed, he is completely defeated.

So here he is down in the pit and, as the angel throws him down there for 1,000 years, he locks and seals it over him. This is an interesting picture. We find satan seized, bound, imprisoned, and cast down into the abyss, and the abyss sealed. It reminds me of what happened to Jesus, who was seized, bound, imprisoned, buried, and a seal put on the stone that covered the tomb. Death, however, could not hold Jesus, and He rose on the third day and is alive forever. Satan, while not able to rise, will be released from the abyss, but just for a short while.

It makes him angry to be released for only a short time after the thousand years are over, after the Kingdom has filled the earth with God's glory, after men have lived under the influence of the Gospel. Not all men will be saved. The Kingdom is bigger than the Church. Not everybody who lives under the influence of the Kingdom will be a member of the Church. Not everyone who walks in the light of the blessing of God that will manifest itself in our world in the last days will be born again. They will experience some kind of influence of sanctity because they are going to walk in the light of the glory of God. It is a little like an unsaved husband who is married to a believing wife. He is sanctified by it (see 1 Cor. 7:14). This does not mean he is born again. It means he gets some of God's blessing because he is married to her.

There is a sense in which unregenerate humanity will get the blessings of the Kingdom not because they are born again, but because they are living under the influence of those who are enjoying Kingdom blessings, because such blessings always overflow. In the generosity of God, He always gives you more than you can contain. But the reason God gives you more than you can cope with is that the overflow blesses somebody else. When the Kingdom comes, the world is full of the peace of God, not because everybody has beaten their swords into plowshares, but because everybody is under the influence of the benefits of God's Kingdom. But there will always be people who, although they enjoy the benefits, actually hate the Kingdom. It is an amazing thing, but there will be those who live under the blessing and despise the blessing, because unregenerate man hates the light and loves the darkness.

So God allows satan to be released for one final fling. But it is only for a short while, only until he is utterly overcome and destroyed. We do not need to live in fear of when that is going to happen. He will come with such lying that if it were possible, he would deceive the saints. But it is not possible. He will lead an army and surround the camp of God, the city God loves. That is not earthly Jerusalem, because the city He loves is the Jerusalem that is from above, that comes down from Heaven from God; it is the Church. The Church is a camp because it is always on pilgrimage, and yet it is a city because it always has a sense of permanence. Satan's great army comes against the heavenly city, against the Church. And God will just slay them in an instant. He will slay them with his breath. He will destroy them with a glance, and it will all be over for the evil one.

It is in this thousand-year period that the saints reign in newness of life, enjoying the first resurrection, having come out of sin and having been seated in the heavenly places with Christ Jesus. As we look at the descriptions of the millennial role of Christ and his risen saints, we are confronted with words and concepts that we are already familiar with. The martyred saints are raised, enthroned, and given authority. This is the first resurrection—when they are raised, by faith in Christ, when they are first born again (see Eph. 2:6). It is in this period that they, with Christ, will bring in the Kingdom and establish His righteousness on the earth. The second resurrection—that of our bodies—takes place at the second coming of Jesus, after the thousand-year rule on earth. We also read here of the second death. Until Jesus comes again, all people will die physically. But at the judgment, unbelievers will be subject to a second death, one of eternal separation from the Lord. There is a simple equation that answers the puzzle of "first resurrection" and "second death" language: born once—die twice; born twice—die once. Those who are born again will not be harmed by the second death.

So, when is the millennium coming? It has already come. When did it begin? It began when satan was bound and when men and women were raised out of sin into the glorious life of the Lord Jesus Christ. This millennium life and rule will grow, increase, brighten, fill the earth with the glory of God, and bring in His Kingdom. Satan will rebel against it, and the rulers of this earth will say, *"Let us break their chains...and throw off their fetters"* (Ps. 2:3). But he who sits in the heavens laughs and says, *"I have installed My King on Zion, My holy hill"* (Ps. 2:6). His anger can flare up in a moment. And for those who rebel, his anger flares up, and they are consumed forever; but the righteous will be forever with the Lord.

CHAPTER 13

The Holy City

Glorious things of thee are spoken, Zion, city of our God.

—John Newton

If you want to read some awesome and breathtaking descriptions of the Holy City, you should look at the Psalms. Many of the Psalms are written to extol the beauty of the city of God. The Psalmists wrote of the literal ancient city of Jerusalem where God dwelt among His people and manifested His glory, from where He sent out His word and established His rule. For example, they remind us that when we come together we ascend the hill of the Lord.

> *Who may ascend the hill of the Lord? Who may stand in His holy place? He who has clean hands and a pure heart* (Psalm 24:3).

And they remind us that we have entered into a rejoicing and committed community, under God's delegated authority.

> *I rejoiced with those who said to me, "Let us go to the house of the Lord." Our feet are standing in your gates, O Jerusalem. Jerusalem is built like a city that is closely compacted together. That is where the tribes go up, the tribes of the Lord, to praise the name of the Lord according to the statute given to Israel. There the thrones for judgment stand, the thrones of the house of David* (Psalm 122:1-5).

The city is "*perfect in beauty*" (Ps. 50:2), "*the joy of the whole earth*" (Ps. 48:2) and the place of which "glorious things are said" (Ps. 87:3). But the city of the psalmists pales into insignificance when compared with this city that comes down out of Heaven from God.

This city is a place of divine judgment, and it is a place of delegated authority. It is a place of glory, of joy, and of holiness—and it is the place where we belong for our citizenship is in Heaven. It does not matter what town you live in; you are a citizen of the heavenly Jerusalem. This city, which has a glorious and wonderful future fulfillment, also has an immediate blessed effect on those who now worship Jesus. We have actually come to the city that Abraham only looked forward to. We have arrived. In fact, so at home are we in this city, so excited are we to be citizens here, so privileged do we feel, that we could say with the Psalmist, "*Better is one day in Your courts than a thousand elsewhere; I would rather be a doorkeeper in the house of my God than dwell in the tents of the wicked*" (Ps. 84:10). He did not mean, of course, that 1,001 days elsewhere might tip the balance! He was saying, "When

I am in Your house, worshiping Your glory, serving Your purpose, I am enjoying a true millennium. I am already a citizen of Your city."

We have already seen that this city is the bride. When we meet as the church, we come to the city of God. The writer to the Hebrews teaches this very clearly. In the twelfth chapter, he tells us that we have not come to Mount Sinai that burns with fire and is covered with smoke; we have not come to the mountain that cannot be touched; we have come to Mount Zion. We have come to the church of the first born, whose names are enrolled in Heaven. We have come to the spirits of righteous men made perfect. We have come to thousands and thousands of angels in festal assembly. We have come to God, the judge of all, for the Church is the place where God's judgments are pronounced. We have come to Jesus, the mediator of a new covenant and to the sprinkled blood that speaks a better word than the blood of Abel (see Hebrews 12:18-24).

Measuring the City

Let me give you an idea of what some authors have written about the new Jerusalem; this illustrates what happens when we take spiritual truths and make a literal interpretation. One wrote something like this: "It appears that the new Jerusalem comes down to the earth, although some believe it will not come all the way down. I believe this city comes to rest upon the new earth because it speaks of it having foundations, and foundations are made for something to rest on. However, some do believe that it will be a sort of sphere suspended in space above the earth."

They begin to postulate the geographical location of the city: will it be on earth, or will it rest suspended above the earth? They hypothesize about its physical shape and size, making statements about the amount of space each of us saints might enjoy as residents of the new Jerusalem, as if we could make these calculations using human imagination and mathematics! They speculate how they might enjoy a view from their apartment houses overlooking the holy city extending as far as the eye could see, from an elevation of 1,500 miles!

To many people this is not only reasonable speculation but something of a test of orthodoxy. So, are we going to be those who interpret these Scriptures literally and turn the measurements into miles, or are we going to be those who understand that God is communicating something to us that is incommunicable, something so wonderful, so vast, so awesome, that words are insufficient to explain it? God uses symbols and signs so that something in our heart and our human intellect will at least catch a glimpse of the glory that is yet to come.

If you have a Bible that does not interpret these things so literally, it will say that the angel measured the city with a rod. Understand that in measuring the holy city we are measuring God's people, just as John measured the worshipers at the altar. The angel measures the city in which the saints of God dwell, and it says he found it to be 12,000 stadia in length and as wide and high as it is long. He measured its wall, and it was 144 cubits thick by the human measurement that the angel was using. Now, when we see these measurements, 12,000 by 144, it should not take a great leap of our understanding to see that he is talking about the habitation of God's redeemed people. It has nothing to do with how many miles wide it is. It has nothing to do with how many square meters you get to live in. It has nothing to do with how high up on the pecking order your apartment is going to be. It has to do simply with this revelation: this is where God's people are!

The Quality of the City

There was a young man in the Book of Zechariah who wanted to go and measure Jerusalem. The angel told him not to measure it, because it was going to be a city without walls. It is limitless. God is not concerned with its size. God is communicating to us Jerusalem's qualities, and they are wonderful qualities. This is how John describes it:

> *It shone with the glory of God, and its brilliance was like that of a very precious jewel, like a jasper, clear as crystal* (Revelation 21:11).

The city looks like a jasper. Do you recall a time when John went into Heaven and saw a throne, and the one who sat upon it shone like a jasper? This city is full of the life and light of the reign of God. When Ezekiel prophesies of a perfect city yet to come and of a temple yet to be established, he is talking about the Church. He is talking of that which is not yet on the earth but will come. He looks down the generations, sees it, and says that the name of the city will be "God is there" (see Ezek. 48:35). The life of this city is vibrant, its glory majestic, its power awesome, its light irresistible, its influence cosmic—for God Himself is there. The Lamb is there. God dwells in this city, and where God dwells, there is glory. In fact, God is the light of this city, and the Lamb is the lamp, and because God and the Lamb have their throne in this city, it shines with the glory of God's throne.

The Scripture tells us that the city has 12 gates and an angel at each gate. Just as the heavenly woman was crowned with 12 stars, so the holy city seems to be crenellated with 12 great gate-towers, and each gate is a single pearl. They are pearls because you have to sell all you have to get in. In a parable that Jesus told, a man was seeking costly pearls. I cannot think of a greater, more costly pearl than the gate that brings me into the city, and I am ready to sell all I have got to get in there. I am ready to give up everything that once was gain to me so that I might gain entrance into the city of God.

It is a pearl because the pain of an oyster creates a pearl, and it is through much tribulation that we will enter the Kingdom. Our suffering, our pains, our irritations are as nothing when I see this great pearl that bids me enter into the presence of the Lamb. As Paul put it, "*For our light and momentary troubles are achieving for us an eternal glory that far outweighs them all*" (2 Cor. 4:17). I may suffer, I may be persecuted, but all that is doing is creating a pearl by which I enter into the city of God.

These 12 gates have written on them the names of the 12 tribes. The walls of this city have 12 foundations, and on them are written the names of the 12 apostles. Chronologically speaking, the patriarchs were here before the apostles, so you would think that the patriarchs would be the foundations and the apostles the means of entrance. That would be a logical and historical way of thinking. How odd, then, that the foundation, which must be laid before a gate can ever be hung, is there before the patriarchs. But you see, the Church is older that Israel. Before there was ever an Israel, before there was ever an Isaac, before there were ever 12 tribes, before there was ever a nation that God called to be his own, there was a record in the heavens upon which were written names, not of those who would belong to the 12 tribes of ethnic Israel, but of those who would belong to the Church of the Lamb. Before God said, "Let there be light," before God called the sun to shine, before God called trees out of the ground or set a man in a garden, there was a book in Heaven called the Lamb's Book of Life, and my name was in it!

You sometimes meet people who struggle with their personal history. You find people who are troubled by the fact that they were abused or abandoned. You find people who continue to suffer from their childhood or teenage years. You find people who still bear the wounds of parental neglect, who feel constantly the pains of rejection. There is an antidote for that. There is a wonderful cure. It is not endless counseling sessions. You can get through the pain because your natural birth was only the means for God to get you born again. Whatever rejection you feel can be lifted because God, in eternity past, had already accepted you. Your name was in the Book of Life before the foundations of the world.

The foundations of this city are all precious stones. Solomon built the temple with costly stones. Paul exhorts those of us who are involved in the ministry of the Church to make sure we build with gold and silver and precious stones. This is the ultimate manifestation of the way God builds. God always builds with that which is of inestimable value. God is not a jerry-builder. God is not a shoddy and dishonest workman. God builds for permanence, and God builds for glory. So the foundations, the very things upon which we stand, which make us strong and give us confidence, are built with jewels. The Garden of Eden was full of jewels. In fact, when you walked through the Garden of Eden you would kick them up with your feet. Ezekiel speaks of the demise of satan and the casting down of the one who was once a servant of God; he tells us that at one time he was in the Garden, once he was on the Holy Mountain. (That is one of the evidences, by the way, that the Garden was on a mountain.) He tells us that he was arrayed with all kinds of precious stones, and he walked among the stones of fire. There were fiery stones all over the ground, and when the sun shone, the jewels—the rubies, the emeralds, the amethyst, and all the costly stones that were just scattered in the dirt of the Garden—sparkled like fire.

Adam walked in such a garden, and when he got home at night, he picked up his foot and said, "What have I here?" He put his fingers between his toes and pulled out an emerald! It reveals to us the costliness of our salvation. We have come to the city that Abraham looked for, and we have discovered it is the most precious of dwelling places.

The foundations of the city are laid out as a square. The Holy City is a cube for this reason: it exactly replicates the Most Holy Place; or perhaps I should say that the Most Holy Place exactly replicates the City. The temple and the tabernacle were only replicating what is now a reality, and it is in the form of a cube. That is why the foundations are laid out as a square.

There are rows that exactly correspond with the breastplate that the High Priest wore. He wore a breastplate of 12 precious stones, and on each one was engraved the name of the tribes of God's people. Now, upon these four square foundation stones are the names of the apostles, and it is a replication of the breastplate that hung over the heart of the High Priest. It tells us that although there is no temple in this city—for the Lamb and He who sits upon the throne are the temple—it is a place of priestly habitation and function.

First, Jesus our great High Priest still carries eternally on his heart the names of his people, for He ever lives to make intercession for us. Like a precious jewel you are on the heart of Jesus. Like a stone of inestimable value you are held close to the beat of his heart. And in this new city we not only stand upon stones, we also enter into the fullness of our priestly function and have stones upon our hearts too, for we have entered into the Melchizedek priesthood, of which Jesus is the eternal High Priest. That is why Paul can speak of "*the grace that was given* [him] *from God, to be a minister of Christ Jesus to the Gentiles, ministering as a priest the gospel of God*" (Rom. 15:15-16 NASB). In this glorious city/temple the people of God enter fully into their dynamic priestly function toward God and the world.

The River of Life

The city has come and revealed itself in all its glory, but God's purposes are not over yet. When John speaks of "a new Heaven and a new earth," he is quoting a passage from Isaiah 65, and if you go back to that passage, it speaks of God making a new Heaven and a new earth and of great blessings that attend those who live in this revolutionary environment. It tells us that in those days weeping will not be heard, infant mortality a thing of the past, and 100-year-olds will be full of vitality and youthfulness. Life will be peaceful, work prosperous, and the environment healed. Fellowship with God will be intimate and spontaneous. And what he is saying is related to everyday life. He is not talking yet about eternity. He is talking about an earthly reality. When this city comes, it will be a "down to earth" city, and the nations will walk by its light, and the nations will bring their glory into it.

As John looked at this city, he saw a river clear as crystal flowing from the throne. It was a river that the prophet Ezekiel, the great prophet of restoration, had previously seen. Ezekiel prophesied as an exile, just as John now prophesies as an exile. Ezekiel prophesied as one in prison just as John is now in prison. Ezekiel prophesied as one carried away from where he longs to be—and so did John. Ezekiel knew that he would never go behind the curtain to fulfill his priesthood, but Heaven was open and he saw visions—just as John did. One of the visions he saw was of the great river of life that flowed from the temple, bringing life everywhere it went.

It was a progressive thing. At first, he was in it up to his ankles, but there was more. Then he was in it up to his knees, but there was more yet. He was in it up to his thighs, but there was more, until he was in it over his head. It was too wide to cross, too deep to stand in. He abandoned himself to the flow of the river. Only at that moment did he see on the banks of the river the tree of life. Not when he was paddling, not when he was wading, but only when he was out of his depth did he see this. We have got to learn to let ourselves get out of our depth in the flow of God's purpose, because that is when the tree of life appears on the banks of the river.

John looked and saw this crystal clear river, and it was running down the middle of the street—an unusual place for a river to be. On either side there were trees of life. It is interesting that when Israel came in to claim the land, to possess that land flowing with milk and honey and to be a radiance of God as a testimony to the ends of the earth, they settled both sides of the River Jordan. Now on both sides of the river there is a tree of life, for food and for the healing of the nations, and it flows crystal clear from the throne. It is all issuing from the authority of Heaven. As God establishes His throne in your life and mine, so rivers of living water will flow from us and heal a world that is a desert and a land that is full of famine. This city truly is the joy of all the earth. This city truly is the hope of every nation. This city surely is the place where we delight to be. We long to flow in the Spirit, even as the waters flowed out of the garden to the four corners of the earth, that the tree of life might be exported to the remotest corners of our world.

This city is coming and has already come. Jesus said,

> *You are the light of the world. A city on a hill cannot be hidden. Neither do people light a lamp and put it under a bowl. Instead they put it on its stand, and it gives light to everyone in the house. In the same way, let your light shine before men, that they may see your good deeds and praise your Father in heaven* (Matthew 5:14-16).

At the beginning of His earthly ministry, Jesus introduced many of the ideas and images that the Book of Revelation expounds—city, hill, lamp stand. He told His disciples that there were prophets who came before them (see Matt. 5:12), implying that they now have the prophetic mantle to continue the purposes of God—and to endure the same persecution as their predecessors. He revealed to them that the lamp enlightens all in the house—a Church full of understanding and truth—and that from the fullness of the house will flow streams of light through words and works so that all men will give glory to God. Our task is to conform our lives to God's Word and reform our congregations into the true city of God that comes down out of Heaven so that we might transform our world to the glory of God. God has purposed that His glory will fill the earth, even as the waters cover the sea. What God has purposed, God will fulfill because His river flows down the middle of the street and God's street is a straight and direct route to His presence. God never built a cul-de-sac. He built a highway with a destination, and the destination is that all of the ends of the earth will see His glory. So let it be. Amen.

Books to help you grow strong in Jesus

THE LION & THE LAMB - VOL. 1

Reflections on the Book of Revelation

By Tony Ling

The Lion & The Lamb is not a typical book on "End Times Events." Rather than making eschatological predictions, it offers wonderful insights that will help you personally to:

- Grasp the Book of Revelation's practical teachings for daily living.
- Steer clear of speculation and overactive imaginations as it sets Revelation firmly among the prophetic writings of the whole Bible.
- Realize the preeminence of Jesus in your life, the triumph of His Kingdom, and an overcoming faith that is truly yours.
- Be encouraged to recognise your true identity.
- Find your ultimate destiny.
- Understand how you can play an important role in advancing the Kingdom of God.

The Lion & The Lamb will affect the way you see your world, enlarge your vision of God's purpose and equip you to be useful for the Master.

ISBN-13: 978-88-89127-39-1